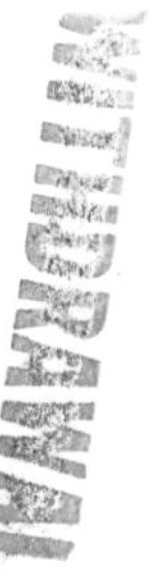

Peter Taylor

Revised Edition

Twayne's United States Authors Series

TUSAS 168

PETER TAYLOR
1917–
Photo by Bill Sublette,
University of Virginia Alumni News

Peter Taylor

Revised Edition

By Albert J. Griffith

Our Lady of the Lake University

Twayne Publishers

A Division of G. K. Hall & Co. • Boston

Peter Taylor, Revised Edition
Albert J. Griffith

Published by Twayne Publishers
A Division of G. K. Hall & Co.
70 Lincoln Street
Boston, Massachusetts 02111

Copyediting supervised by Barbara Sutton
Book production by Gabrielle B. McDonald
Book design by Barbara Anderson

Typeset in 11 pt. Garamond
by Compositors Corporation, Cedar Rapids, Iowa

Printed on permanent/durable acid-free paper
and bound in the United States of America

First published 1990
10 9 8 7 6 5 4 3 2 1

Library of Congress Cataloging-in-Publication Data
Griffith, Albert J. (Albert Joseph), 1932–
Peter Taylor / by Albert J. Griffith. — Rev. ed.
p. cm. — (Twayne's United States authors series ; TUSAS 168)
Includes bibliographical references.
ISBN 0-8057-7549-8
1. Taylor, Peter Hillsman, 1917– —Criticism and interpretation.
I. Title. II. Series.
PS3539.A9633Z7 1990
813′.54—dc20 89-38329
CIP

For Elizabeth

Contents

About the Author

Albert J. Griffith is professor of English at Our Lady of the Lake University, San Antonio, Texas. A native of Fort Worth, Texas, he received his B.A. from St. Edward's University and his M.A. and Ph.D. from the University of Texas at Austin. At Our Lady of the Lake University he has served as chair of the English Department, director of the humanities division, vice president for development and public relations, and vice president and dean of academic affairs. He has been a member of the board of directors of the National Council of Teachers of English and has served on various committees of the San Antonio Council of Teachers of English, the Texas Joint Council of Teachers of English, the Conference of College Teachers of English of Texas, and the South Central Modern Language Association. His work has appeared in various periodicals and literary and critical anthologies. In addition to his pioneering study of Peter Taylor, he has published articles on such Southern writers as Eudora Welty, Carson McCullers, and Flannery O'Connor; his other scholarly work includes publications or papers on Hawthorne, linguistics, cinema, humor, and learning assessment. In 1988 he was named a Piper Professor by the Minnie Stevens Piper Foundation in recognition of excellence in teaching.

Preface

Peter Taylor has garnered some of the highest critical acclaim of any writer of his generation, but he has never been obsessed with fame and fortune. "I've always had a lot of appreciative literary friends, and maybe that meant more to me than it should have," he says, "but it's all chance whether or not you become known in your generation. My concern is with how good what I write is and with the opinion of my peers."[1]

When the first edition of this book was written some two decades ago, Peter Taylor had already been lauded as "a new major writer of American fiction," "possibly the most interesting and accomplished new writer to come out of the South," "an impeccable stylist," "an authentic genius," and "a perceptive artist, a skillful craftsman, and . . . the only American of his generation whose work can stand comparisons with that of Frank O'Connor and Chekhov and Joyce."[2] He was nevertheless hardly known at all to the general public, and of his seven published books—five collections of short stories, one novella, and one play—only the most recent (*Collected Stories* [1969]) was still in print. He seemed destined to stay in that limbo reserved for short story writers who never produce a major novel.

Since then, however, he has published five more books, including the Pulitzer Prize-winning novel *A Summons to Memphis* (1986). In the last ten years, in addition to the Pulitzer, he has been awarded the Gold Medal for Literature of the American Academy and Institute of Arts and Letters, the PEN/Faulkner Award and the Ritz Hemingway Prize for fiction, and a Senior Fellowship from the National Endowment for the Arts. The most ironic of all the belated recognitions came in August 1987 when the editors of *Esquire* magazine in their every-quarter-of-a-century "Guide to the Literary Universe" listed seventy-year-old Peter Taylor, after a full fifty years of publishing, as a "Rising Star" on the literary horizon.[3]

Readers of this revised edition, therefore, are not only more likely to be already familiar with Taylor's distinguished reputation, they are also considerably more likely to be able to get their hands on his books, since most of his work is now back in print, much of it in inexpensive paperback as well as hardcover. This edition's purpose, then, is not so much to introduce the work of a brilliant but relatively unknown writer as it is to provide an overview of the unity and integrity of a major author's canon—a canon that covers half a century, three distinct genres, and a goodly number of the deepest secrets of the human heart. Although there are now other books providing primary and secondary bibliographies, a collection of interviews, and explications of selected stories, this Twayne's United States Authors Series volume is still the only comprehensive study of Taylor's total work.

Space limitations have made it necessary to cut back on some of the discussion in the first edition in order to make room for coverage of the new work of the last twenty years. In general, though, I have elected to provide more detailed analyses of earlier works where characteristic themes or techniques are first introduced, even though that has meant that certain later works of equal or even greater significance must be given shorter shrift. Since Taylor's work is almost uniformly of high literary merit, I have also thought it wiser to use my limited space more for descriptive analysis (with rather free use of direct quotation) than for elaboration of my own critical opinions and preferences.

(To avoid unnecessary and obtrusive documentation, parenthetical page citations for Taylor's primary works are given in the text only for quotations of one hundred words or more. Since many of Taylor's works appear in more than one collection, page citations are given for each volume in which the work appears. The text of the quotation, however, is taken from the earliest book publication of the work—except for *A Woman of Means,* for which the 1983 reprint is used.)

Peter Taylor, who has eschewed the writing of criticism himself ever since he wrote a review of Allen Tate's *The Fathers* while he was still an undergraduate, has well expressed the fundamental inadequacy of the critic's task: "I have a horror of defining, of limiting. Everything seems to me to be such a cliché as soon as I say it. And the other thing is, as soon as I make a point, I am sure I can disprove it, am sure that the opposite is also true!"[4]

Exactly! And there are so many other truths to be stated about work as rich and rewarding as Taylor's that this volume will have accomplished its purpose if it does nothing more than lead readers back to a "rising star" whose light, powerful as it is, has only begun to be felt in the literary universe.

Albert J. Griffith

Our Lady of the Lake University

Acknowledgments

I am greatly indebted to Peter Taylor, who has given me permission to quote from his works and who has graciously assisted me in assembling some of the biographical information.

For other kind assistance, I am grateful to Hubert H. McAlexander, J. H. E. Paine, Stuart Wright, Janice Delaney, Lois Green, David Lytle, Antoinette Garza, Carmen Garcia, and the administration of Our Lady of the Lake University.

A portion of Chapter Eight is a revised version of my article "Presences, Absences, and Peter Taylor's Plays," copyright © 1977 by Washington and Lee University, reprinted from *Shenandoah: The Washington and Lee University Review* with the permission of the Editor.

I wish to make acknowledgment also to the following:

To Astor-Honor, Inc. for permission to quote from *Tennessee Day in St. Louis,* copyright © 1955, 1956, 1957 by Peter Taylor; from "The Dark Walk" in *The Widows of Thornton,* copyright © 1948, 1949, 1950, 1951, 1954 by Peter Taylor; and from "An Overwhelming Question," "Sky Line," and "A Strange Story" in *Miss Leonora When Last Seen,* copyright © 1948, 1949, 1950, 1951, 1954, 1960, 1961, 1963 by Peter Taylor. Reprinted by permission of Astor-Honor, Inc., New York, N.Y. 10017.

To Frederic C. Beil, Publisher for permission to quote from *A Woman of Means,* copyright © 1950, 1983 by Peter Taylor, and from *A Stand in the Mountains,* copyright © 1985 by Peter Taylor.

To Doubleday & Co., Inc. for permission to quote from Peter Taylor, *The Old Forest and Other Stories,* published by Dial Press, copyright © 1941, 1945, 1947, 1949, 1951, 1958, 1959, 1979, 1981, 1985 by Peter Taylor.

To Farrar, Straus and Giroux, Inc. for: Excerpts from *The Collected Stories of Peter Taylor.* Copyright © 1940, 1941, 1948, 1949, 1950, 1951, 1955, 1957, 1958, 1959, 1960, 1961, 1962, 1963, 1964, 1967, 1968, 1969. Copyright renewed © 1967, 1968 by Peter Taylor. Reprinted by permission of Farrar, Straus and Giroux, Inc.

To Alfred A. Knopf, Inc. for permission to quote from Peter Taylor, *A Summons to Memphis,* copyright © 1986 by Peter Taylor, and from "The Captain's Son," "The Hand of Emmagene," "Her Need," "In the Miro District," "The Instruction of a Mistress," and "Three Heroines" from Peter Taylor, *In the Miro District and Other Stories,* copyright © 1974, 1975, 1976, 1977 by Peter Taylor.

To *The Paris Review* for permission to quote from Barbara Thompson, "Interview with Peter Taylor," originally published as "The Art of Fiction XCIX: Peter Taylor," *The Paris Review* 29 (Fall 1987): 45–82, copyright © 1987 by *The Paris Review.*

To University Press of Mississippi for quotations from Hubert H. McAlexander, "A Composite Conversation with Peter Taylor," *Conversations with Peter Taylor,* ed. Hubert H. McAlexander, copyright © 1987 by University Press of Mississippi. Reprinted by permission.

To Washington and Lee University for quotations from Stephen Goodwin, "An Interview with Peter Taylor." Copyright © 1973 by Washington and Lee University, reprinted from *Shenandoah: The Washington and Lee University Review* with the permission of the Editor.

Chronology

1917 Peter Hillsman Taylor born 8 January in Trenton, Tennessee, on ninth wedding anniversary of his parents, Matthew Hillsman Taylor (1884–1965) and Katherine Baird (Taylor) Taylor (1886–1969).

1924 Family moves from Trenton to Nashville.

1926 Family moves to St. Louis where father soon becomes president of Missouri State Life Insurance Company. Attends Miss Rossman's School.

1929 Attends St. Louis Country Day School.

1932 Family moves to Memphis. Attends Memphis Central High School.

1935 After graduation, works way to England on freighter.

1936 Takes courses under Allen Tate at Southwestern University at Memphis in spring. Starts at Vanderbilt University in fall under John Crowe Ransom; becomes friend of Randall Jarrell.

1937 Drops out of college and sells real estate (after Ransom moves to Kenyon College). First two stories in *River.* Begins reviewing for Memphis *Commercial-Appeal.*

1938 Enters Kenyon in fall. Rooms with Robert Lowell. Begins contributing stories and poems to student publication.

1939 Poem in *Kenyon Review.*

1940 Graduates in spring. Briefly enrolls in fall for graduate work under Robert Penn Warren and Cleanth Brooks at Louisiana State University. "A Spinster's Tale" in *Southern Review.*

1941 Enters U.S. Army in June (serves at Fort Oglethorpe, Georgia, and later at Tidworth Camp in England).

1943 Marries poet Eleanor Ross (b. 1920) of Norwood, North Carolina, at Monteagle, Tennessee, on 4 June.

1945 Discharged from Army as sergeant on 20 December. *Partisan Review* award to "The Scoutmaster."

1946 Teaches at Women's College of University of North Carolina at Greensboro, after brief job with New York publisher.

1947 Buys Greensboro duplex with Jarrell. Buys old Hillsboro farmhouse (first of many old home renovation projects).

1948 First book, *A Long Fourth,* in March. First child, Katherine Baird Taylor, born 30 September. First story in *New Yorker,* 6 November. Assistant professor, Indiana University.

1949 Returns to faculty post at Greensboro.

1950 *A Woman of Means.* Guggenheim Fellowship for 1950–51.

1952 Teaches at University of Chicago in spring. National Institute of Arts and Letters award. Begins associate professorship at Kenyon in fall.

1953 Begins six-year advisory editorship of *Kenyon Review.*

1954 *The Widows of Thornton.*

1955 Son, Peter Ross Taylor, born 7 February. Fulbright grant to do research in Paris in 1955–56. Lectures at Fourth Conference on American Studies at Oxford.

1957 *Tennessee Day in St. Louis.* Premiere at Kenyon 24–27 April. Associate professor Ohio State University (January to June each year). Lectures at Chicago and Vanderbilt.

1958 Summer and fall in Italy.

1959 *Happy Families Are All Alike.* O. Henry first prize for "Venus, Cupid, Folly, and Time." Buys house in Monteagle.

1960 Eleanor Taylor's *Wilderness of Ladies.* Ohioana Book Award to *Happy Families.* Ford Foundation Fellowship at London's Royal Court Theatre for 1960–61 academic year.

1962 *Sewanee Review* special issue on Taylor (Autumn).

1963 Rejoins University of North Carolina at Greensboro.

1964 *Miss Leonora When Last Seen.* Visiting professor at Harvard in fall.

1966 Rockefeller Foundation grant provides 1966–67 sabbatical.

1967 *Randall Jarrell, 1914–1965* (coeditor). Professor of English, University of Virginia. *Critique* special issue.

1968 *A Stand in the Mountains* in *Kenyon Review.*

1969 Inducted into National Institute of Arts and Letters. *Collected Stories.*

1972 Founders Day Address at University of South 10 October; Litt.D. degree. Eleanor Taylor's *Welcome Eumenides.*

1973 *Presences: Seven Dramatic Pieces.* Visiting professor at Harvard, fall semester.

1974 Suffers heart attack.

1977 *In the Miro District. Shenandoah* special issue.

1978 Gold Medal Award for short story from American Academy and Institute of Arts and Letters.

1983 Inducted into American Academy of Arts and Letters in May. Retires from University of Virginia in June. Eleanor Taylor's *New and Selected Poems.*

1984 *A Woman of Means* (reprint). $25,000 senior fellowship from National Endowment for the Arts. "The Old Forest" filmed.

1985 *The Old Forest.* Visiting professor at University of Georgia, spring. Southern Writers Conference, Chattanooga, 22–23 February.

1986 PEN/Faulkner Award for *The Old Forest.* Suffers stroke 24 July. *A Stand in the Mountains,* revised. *A Summons to Memphis.* Withdraws self from American Book Award competition.

1987 Ritz Hemingway Prize for fiction. Pulitzer Prize for *A Summons to Memphis. Conversations with Peter Taylor. Journal of the Short Story in English* special issue.

1988 Founding member of Fellowship of Southern Writers.

Chapter One

The Measure of Peter Taylor's World

"Tennessee Is a State of Mind"

His native state of Tennessee is a subject that has held a lifelong fascination for Peter Taylor. "I consider the fiction I have written merely a by-product of my efforts to understand who and what I am," Taylor has said. "My feelings are both that this region of the upper South is very much a part of me and that I am very much a part of it. Why a writer should be so egotistical as to have such feelings about a whole region and so crass as to express these feelings is a mystery. But nearly everything about art is a mystery and must ever be so, and yet this is my mystery, so to speak, and worries me more than most of the other mysteries of life."[1]

Clearly the most important single element in Peter Taylor's Tennessee background is the small country town where he was born—for out of that county town came the traditional values and genteel manners that have dominated his responses to the mystery of life. That town is Trenton, Tennessee, known for little more than the pastoral serenity of its maple-lined streets. Located in the old Chickasaw country of West Tennessee, Trenton is the county seat of Gibson County and a local trading center for the cotton, tomato, and strawberry farmers of the area; Taylor's father and paternal grandfather practiced law together there. Trenton is the obvious model for Taylor's fictional town of Thornton, the point of origin of numerous characters in more than a dozen of Taylor's works, and it no doubt also contributes some features to the imaginary towns of Lovell, Braxton, Thomasville, and Blackwell in other stories.

Peter Taylor lived in Trenton only seven years. Born 8 January 1917, on the ninth anniversary of his parents' wedding, he was the youngest of the four children of Matthew Hillsman and Katherine Baird (Taylor) Taylor and the one who would have the least contact with his place of origin. The family moved first to Nashville in 1924, then to St. Louis, Missouri, in 1926, and finally to Memphis in 1932. "No matter where we lived after we left

Trenton, . . . we nearly always went back to Trenton for holidays," Taylor has recalled in his loving reminiscence, "Tennessee Caravan, 1920–1940." "It was those departures and arrivals on those visits that seem to me now the most exciting events of my little-boyhood and early adolescence. Or, rather, the *next* most exciting. The *most* exciting, I suppose, were the removals themselves when we went to take up residence in a new place. Our removals were done always in the most thoroughgoing manner and on the grandest scale. We left behind not a sheet of paper or a picture or a single stick of Mother's heavy, mid-Victorian furniture. Every keepsake in the attic, every old toy any of us children ever had, every coal scuttle or garden tool in the cellar went with us."[2] Of course, what the family also brought along in those moves was a great deal of cultural baggage—old roles and customs that could only produce ambivalence and conflict in the less congenial settings to which they were transported.

Such old patterns of behavior, inherited from the country town, were rapidly giving way to new ones in the large urban centers where Taylor spent his formative years. Perhaps the most important phase of his life—the period between the ages of nine and fifteen—was spent not in the South at all, but in the Midwestern metropolis of St. Louis. "To my brother and sisters, as to my parents, the period in St. Louis represents a relatively brief interlude in their lives," Taylor makes his narrator say in "The End of Play," one of his still-uncollected stories. "They are vague about a lot of things that are very clear in my mind and they will ask me to refresh their memories about people and addresses and even events that took place in that period. For me, of course, almost the reverse is true since I lived there during those years of life when one is taking his measure of the world."[3] In an interview Taylor has described two of the most "haunting" images of his childhood: the image of a cleared site in Trenton where his father had once planned to build a house before his move and the image of "a great hole in the earth" where "a huge, grand house" the family had once lived in in St. Louis had been torn down—images of "the life that was never to be and the life that could never be again."[4]

That kind of fascination with time and change may help to explain the peculiar mixture of sentiment and irony through which Peter Taylor envisions life in his fiction. The migration of rural Southerners to the cities and of urban Southerners out of the South clearly did not cut them off from their roots. As so many of Taylor's own works depict, Southern families in exile carried with them as much as they could of the manners and mores of their old way of life. Often bringing along their black servants and dependent kinfolks, transplanted Southern gentry would try to live their old roles in their new environments, making only minimal adaptations and ignoring unpleasant incongruities. Taylor has one of his characters in *Tennessee Day in St. Louis* preparing a speech entitled "Tennessee Is a State of Mind." That phrase is a particularly apt summary of the lasting influence of Southern culture on those who have once experienced it. "Ah, sometimes," the same Taylor character observes, "the Southerners one meets out of the South seem more Southern than the South." Always in the memories of these exiles, at any rate, was the image of the rural society on which they based what certainties they still retained.

Taylor's own family unquestionably had a vivid past to remember. Both of his grandfathers were lawyers and politicians, and both, coincidentally, were named Robert Taylor. The more famous of the two was his mother's father, Robert Love ("Bob") Taylor of Happy Valley, Tennessee, a legend in his own lifetime. A United States congressman (1879–81), a three-term governor of the state (1887–89, 1889–91, and 1897–99), and finally a United States senator (1907–1912), Bob Taylor was a practical joker, a renowned spinner of tall tales, and a wily vote-getter—all in the tradition of another eminent Tennesseean, Davy Crockett. Governor Bob's most famous campaign was the 1886 race for the governorship, which found him, as the Democratic nominee, pitted against his brother, Alf Taylor, the Republican nominee. To this day, wry stories are still told about the two brothers stumping the state together, telling tales, fiddling, and pulling tricks on each other, in what came to be called Tennessee's "War of the Roses." An interesting footnote to this bit of Taylor family history is the fact that the prohibition cause also had a token candidate for governor that year: former Congressman and former Commissioner of Indian Affairs Nathaniel Green Taylor—Peter Taylor's great-grandfather, the father of Bob and Alf. And, while Bob was the victor in 1886, Alf Taylor had his turn as governor thirty-five years later when he was seventy-three and had already served three terms as United States congressman. Governor Bob died five years before Peter Taylor was born, but Governor Alf lived till 1931 when his grandnephew was fourteen. Probably stories about the one and recollections of the other contributed heavily to Peter Taylor's characterizations of Senator Caswell in *Tennessee Day in St. Louis,* to the imagined convention delegate in "The End of Play," to the governor/senator grandfather in "The Megalopolitans," and to the deceased senator whose funeral cortege is the central event in the work-in-progress, *To the Lost State.*

Peter Taylor's father, Hillsman Taylor, also had a political career as a young man. Just three years after his graduation from Vanderbilt Law School, he served as speaker of the Tennessee House of Representatives. He was attorney general of the Thirteenth Judicial Circuit of Tennessee at the time Peter was born. When he moved his family to St. Louis in 1926, interests other than politics took on new importance. "We all came here to make money, you know, and came of our own free will," one of Peter Taylor's St. Louis characters says of the Southern families transplanted to the Midwest.

Hillsman Taylor, too, became a successful businessman in the big city. It was in St. Louis that the former country lawyer soon became president of the Missouri State Life Insurance Company and, as one of his major accomplishments, negotiated what was said to be the largest reinsurance deal of that day, involving three hundred million dollars worth of insurance and thirty-nine million dollars worth of assets. Later, he was to realize that a close friend and business partner had gotten him to go to St. Louis just so he couldn't see the "very crooked things" the partner was doing in Nashville. That friend and partner was Rogers Caldwell, the "J. P. Morgan of the South," who built "a gigantic financial empire which, before it fell in 1930, was worth about one-half billion dollars"; when it collapsed "no less than 120 banks in seven southern states went down . . ., while numerous others merged in desperation with stronger banks."[5] "After that," Peter Taylor recalls, "my father said he would never live in the same town as Rogers Caldwell, and we didn't mention his name."[6] Hillsman Taylor's "betrayal" is, of course, the inspiration for George Carver's similar betrayal by Lewis Shackleford in *A Summons to Memphis* (and, to a lesser extent, for the betrayal incidents in "Dean of Men").

In the uncollected story "Uncles" Peter Taylor has a young artistically inclined hero concerned that the "deadly practical things" of the business world that men were caught up in seemed to rule out "everything clever, gentle, and light" from the world that women—and artists—lived in.[7] Certainly in his own life Peter was often at loggerheads with his father, although as aging changed both father and son he was able to be "much softer, easier" on at least some of the father figures in his later fiction than he was on earlier characters of that type.[8] At any rate, his mother was a counterbalancing influence in his life; he confesses to adoring her from the day he was born—and considers himself lucky that she spared him from the ruined life "that is often the fate of little boys who adore their mothers" by sensibly rejecting his adoration and paying him no more attention than she did the other children.[9] Many times Peter Taylor has attributed his narrative propensity to the Southern oral tradition his mother preserved, and he dedicated his *Collected Stories* to her as "the best teller of tales I know . . . from whose lips I first heard many of the stories in this book." As he focused on the lives of Southern women in many of his early stories (not out of any "conscious philosophy" but simply because he had such a store of women's stories to tell), he came to see "that certain people were always getting the short end." "I found the Blacks being exploited by white women, and the white women being exploited by the white men," he has said. "In my stories that always came through to me and from the stories themselves I began to understand what I really thought."[10]

That remarkable statement demonstrates the degree to which Taylor's artistic sensibility liberated him from the race, class, and gender biases that his privileged upbringing might have fostered. The kind of life Taylor knew in Nashville, St. Louis, and Memphis can be inferred from the many stories in which he depicts families of similar status and affluence.[11] For the children in such families there are few hardships and many luxuries, including summer vacations in Michigan, dancing classes, gala parties, expensive gifts, and, of course, an ample supply of black servants. Only the Great Depression could put a slight damper on their generally optimistic outlook. "If you were a worrier, as I was," one of Taylor's young protagonists says in "The Other Times," "it didn't seem possible that you would ever be able to make a living of the kind your father had always made." And in the background, associated with just such fears of failure, was the memory of the country town from which the family came and to which it might someday have to return.

His Southern agrarian heritage has thus always loomed large in Taylor's imagination. It has been, however, a burden as much as a birthright. It has also been like a legacy held in trust—something he could use but not fully possess and certainly not dispose of. And, as a result, Peter Taylor has been, of all the brilliant talents of the Southern Literary Renaissance, the one most capable of seeing Southern culture simultaneously both as insider and outsider.

But inside or outside his native state, Peter Taylor's state of mind has always remained Tennessee.

The Making of a Writer

Hillsman Taylor had received his law degree from Vanderbilt University in 1906 and he hoped that his younger son would follow in his footsteps. That young son, however, had his own ideas about his education. After attending Miss Rossman's private school in St. Louis and St. Louis Country Day School, Peter Taylor graduated from Memphis Central High School in 1935 with a scholarship to Columbia University, where he hoped to study writing. A most unpleasant quarrel ensued; father and son stopped speaking; and son Peter, refusing to give in, that summer worked his way to England on a freighter and in the fall took a job at the Memphis *Commercial-Appeal.*

In the spring of 1936 Taylor finally enrolled in some English courses at Southwestern at Memphis. His instructor was poet Allen Tate—whom Taylor later described as "the best teacher I ever had," who "made literature and ideas seem more important than anything else in the world, [so that] you wanted to put everything else aside and follow him."[12] Some forty years later Tate was to express an equally admiring assessment of his pupil: "I was Peter's first college English teacher, but I found I could not teach him anything so I asked him to leave the class after about two weeks. The simple truth is that he did not need to know anything I could teach him. He had a perfection of style at the age of 18 that I envied."[13] Unfortunately, Tate left to take a special lectureship in modern poetry at Columbia the very next year; but he advised his young protégé to go to the school his father had picked. There, at Vanderbilt, Taylor would have the opportunity to study under Tate's old mentor, John Crowe Ransom, the founder of the Fugitive group and the dean of the New Critics.

Taylor went on to Vanderbilt that fall, but he was doomed to another disappointment when Ransom moved the following year to Kenyon College in Gambier, Ohio. Virtually dropping out of college for a year (he took only a few courses as a special student at Southwestern), Taylor took a job selling real estate in Memphis. Not until the fall of 1938 did he transfer to Kenyon and resume his study under Ransom. Because he did badly in mathematics, a part of the prelaw curriculum, he was finally allowed by his father to concentrate his studies in literature.[14]

By the time he graduated from Kenyon in 1940, Taylor already had published nine poems, eight short stories, and a chapter from a novel in progress in the Kenyon student publication, a poem in the Ransom-edited *Kenyon Review,* and two short stories in the Oxford, Mississippi, literary magazine *River.* He next tried graduate work at Louisiana State University, studying under Robert Penn Warren and Cleanth Brooks. By this time, however, he knew his vocation was to be a fiction writer rather than a scholar, and he dropped his coursework and finished the year just reading and writing. Warren, who had earlier turned down the two stories accepted by *River,* now took three of Taylor's stories ("A Spinster's Tale," "Sky Line," and "The Fancy Woman") for the *Southern Review,* and the literary career of Peter Taylor was officially launched.

During these apprenticeship years Taylor had some into contact with some of the most original and stimulating critical and creative minds in America. Since three of the most important of these—Ransom, Tate, and Warren—were leaders of the Agrarian movement, it is surprising that so little evidence of Agrarian thinking is found in Taylor's work. One early story, "The Party" (1937), attempts to contrast the pastoral ideal so dear to the Agrarians with the urban-industrial reality, but it is an immature and mawkish story. Another story, "A Long Fourth" (1946), depicts two Southern characters deliberately burlesquing the Agrarian line to the embarrassment of a Yankee visitor. Of course, there are throughout Taylor's work many wistful references to "the old ways and the old teachings," to "the standards of a past era, a better era," to the former "atmosphere of a prosperous and civilized existence," and to the present sad corruption for the "traditions and institutions" of the country. But these are not direct comments by the author; they are reflections of the thoughts of various characters, many of whom would gladly rally with the Agrarians against the urban-industrial menace. Taylor himself usually stands apart, not judging. He does, however, in "Miss Leonora When Last Seen" allow his gentle irony to prick those who "go on having sweet dreams" about preserving unspoilt the little country towns in which they themselves never actually live.

Ransom, Tate, and Warren undoubtedly had more influence on Taylor as literary critics and theorists than they had as Agrarians. As proponents of the New Criticism, all three were making important contributions to a revolution in literary study at the very time Taylor had them as teachers. Tate's *Reactionary Essays on Poetry and Ideas,* for instance, appeared in 1936, the year Taylor was taking his courses at Southwestern. One of Ransom's most important critical works, *The World's Body,* was published in 1938, the year Taylor followed him to Kenyon. And Brooks and Warren's landmark textbook *Understanding Poetry* was introduced to college classrooms in 1938 and was making its first big impact about the time Taylor enrolled in Louisiana State.

Henry James, of course, was the patron saint of all the New Critics, and Taylor must have been amply exposed to both Jamesian theory and Jamesian practice by his literary mentors. In *The House of Fiction,* a 1950 short story anthology, for example, Tate and his wife Caroline Gordon take their title and their epigraph from James, include stories by James and several Jamesian disciples, base their analyses of the stories on James's theories, and pack their bibliography with books by and about James. It is no wonder, then, that in the highly autobiographical story "1939" Taylor depicts his young Kenyon College hero as writing obvious imitations of Henry James, or that Taylor would himself several times confess that his play *Missing Person,* from *Presences,* his collection of James-like ghost plays, was an unconscious "steal" from James's "The Jolly Corner." No wonder, either, that Taylor's very Jamesian book, *The Widows of Thornton,* should be dedicated to those disciples of the master, "Allen and Caroline."

Leo Tolstoy, Anthony Trollope, Thomas Mann, James Joyce, D. H. Lawrence, Marcel Proust, William Faulkner, and Frank O'Connor are other writers whose influence Taylor has candidly acknowledged. But it took the combination of a classic Russian novelist, Ivan Turgenev, and a slick American popular writer of the 1930s, Margaret Ayer Barnes, to make him discover he could write about his own background: their works were "about people somewhat like my own family, and it just electrified me that you could write stories about them."[15] And perhaps more important than any other influence from his reading is Anton Chekhov, to whom Taylor is most frequently compared and from whom he admits learning to "examine things from all sides" (even while he sees himself as lacking Chekhov's great "poetic talent").[16]

Taylor has also frequently acknowledged how lucky he was to have a supportive circle of literary friends who responded enthusiastically to his work during the many years he remained virtually unknown to the general public. At Kenyon, Ransom arranged that his literary students—all eleven of them—could live together in Douglass House, a small residence on Kenyon's Middle Path. "It may be," Taylor says, "that the most any of us learned at Kenyon was what we learned from each other."[17] Taylor's Kenyon circle included poet Randall Jarrell, whom he had first met at Vanderbilt, and poet Robert Lowell, who was his Douglass House roommate. The three became lifelong friends: Lowell went to Louisiana State with Taylor, served as best man at his wedding, and dedicated several poems to him; Jarrell introduced Taylor to New York publishing, worked with him and shared a duplex with him at Greensboro, North Carolina, and became the chief mentor in the poetic career of Taylor's wife Eleanor; and Taylor remained the stable and stalwart "normal" friend that the two befrenzied poets could count on through their various marriages and turbulent bouts with mental illness.[18]

When Taylor married Eleanor Lily Ross of Norwood, North Carolina, in 1943 (just six weeks after Allen Tate and Caroline Gordon introduced them), he found himself in the middle of another literary circle—"the writing Rosses of North Carolina"—for not only was Eleanor herself a poet, her two brothers (James Ross and Fred Ross) were novelists, her sister (Jean Ross Justice) was a short story writer, and her brother-in-law (Donald Justice) was a poet.[19] (No wonder, then, that the Taylor's own two children, Katherine Baird Taylor and [Peter] Ross Taylor, became, respectively, a short story writer and a poet.)

Also numbered among Taylor's literary friends are such prominent figures as fiction writers Jean Stafford (Lowell's first wife), Katherine Anne Porter, Eudora Welty, Andrew Lytle, J. F. Powers, and Robie Macauley, as well as poets Robert Fitzgerald, John Thompson, James Merrill, Richard Wilbur, John Ciardi, and James Boatright. Protégés from Taylor's creative writing classes include such promising talents as Stephen Goodwin, Thomas Molyneux, James Alan McPherson, John Casey, and Robert Wilson.

"The fact is," Taylor said in his acceptance speech upon receiving the Gold Medal for fiction from the American Academy and Institute of Arts and Letters in 1979, "that I have always had a wide circle of highly intelligent, greatly gifted literary friends whom I have respected and whose respect I have enjoyed, and that has been the kind of glory I have had . . . . I have somehow found my glory and satisfaction in that circle of friends."[20]

"Making Sense of Life"

In the story "1939" Taylor's first-person narrator depicts himself as a college teacher and writer who has enjoyed neither great financial success nor an extravagant literary reputation. "I stand before the class as a kind of journeyman writer, a type of whom Trollope might have approved," he says. "Yet this man behind the lectern is a man who seems happy in the knowledge that he knows—or thinks he knows—what he is about." Probably no better summation of Taylor's own literary self-image could be given. From the start, he has known what he was about, and he never seems to have complained about his reception as an artist.

Over and over again in interviews Taylor has made it clear he does not like the term "professional writer": he equates it with "careerist"—someone who focuses on the rewards of fame and money instead of on the creation of the work of art. For him, writing is something much more special than producing on demand whatever the current fashion calls for or the existing market will buy; he writes not because he has to turn out a book each year, but out of a "compulsion" to deal with the particular matter that inspires a given work. His vision of his craft is highly idealistic:

> I think trying to write is a religious exercise. You are trying to understand life, and you can only get the illusion of doing it fully by writing. That is, it's the only way I can come to understand things fully. When I create, when I put my own mark on something and form it, I begin to know the whole truth about it, how it was put together. Then you can begin to change things around. You know all this after you have written a lot. You really know. And it has become the most important thing in your life. It has nothing to do with craft, or even art, in a way. It is making sense of life. It is coming to understand yourself.[21]

There is little doubt that Taylor's career has been faithfully and consistently directed to this personal artistic ideal.

The early start Taylor got when he began publishing as an undergraduate was offset to some extent by the hiatus created by World War II. Taylor entered the United States Army as an enlisted man in June 1941 and served two and a half years at Fort Oglethorpe, Georgia (the setting for "Rain in the Heart"), before going overseas to Tidworth Camp in England. Assigned to the Rail Transportation Corps, Taylor avoided officers candidate school but rose to the rank of sergeant before his honorable discharge in December 1945. He then worked briefly as a reader for Henry Holt publishing house in New York before turning to the teaching of creative writing as a livelihood.

Taylor's first academic post was at the Woman's College of the University of North Carolina at Greensboro in fall 1946. Three times he returned to the Greensboro school after teaching stints elsewhere: at Indiana University, 1948–49; at the University of Chicago, 1952, Kenyon College, 1952–57, and Ohio State University, 1957–63; and at Harvard University, 1964. From 1967 to his retirement in 1983 he held an endowed professorship in the writing program at the University of Virginia, teaching just half a year (except in 1973 when he taught the other half of the year at Harvard). Since his retirement he has taken on occasional teaching, such as a visiting professorship at the University of Georgia in 1985. Overall, Taylor seems to have found his academic work compatible with his artistic goals: "When you're a writer, you're by yourself all the time, and you get withdrawn from the world. Teaching draws you out. I'm a gregarious person who likes to see people."[22]

Although Taylor published one or two minor stories during the war years, it was only between 1945 and 1947 that he hit his stride with stories in *Sewanee Review, Partisan Review,* and *Kenyon Review.* Between the end of the war and the publication of his first short story collection, *A Long Fourth,* in 1948, he had also written two plays and a "long novelette." The critical reception to *A Long Fourth* was encouraging, so the novelette was published in 1950, under the title *A Woman of Means.* Very important to his career was his association with the *New Yorker,* which published some twenty-six Peter Taylor stories between 1948 and 1981. Taylor followed *A Long Fourth* with six more story collections: three contained all new stories (*The Widows of Thornton,* 1954; *Happy Families Are All Alike,* 1959; *In the Miro District,* 1977) and three were mixtures of new and previously collected stories (*Miss Leonora When Last Seen,* 1963; *Collected Stories,* 1969; *The Old Forest,* 1985). Two full-length plays, *Tennessee Day in St. Louis* and *A Stand in the Mountains,* were published in book form in 1957 and 1986, respectively, and a collection of one-act ghost plays, *Presences: Seven Dramatic Pieces,* appeared in 1973. Finally, in 1986, after resisting the pressure for half a century, Taylor published his first full-fledged novel, *A Summons to Memphis.*

An unspectacular but steady pile of accolades began to accumulate over the years as Taylor's literary reputation slowly grew. Critical attention was fairly sparse for his early works, but each book received almost unanimous praise from those reviewers who did take notice; his last three story collections and *A Summons to Memphis* were both widely and favorably attended to. Taylor stories were frequently chosen for the *Best American Short Stories* and O. Henry prize-story annuals, with one story ("Venus, Cupid, Folly, and Time") being included in both of the 1959 annuals and even winning the O. Henry first prize. Other honors included a *Partisan Review* award for "The Scoutmaster" in 1945 and the Ohioana Book Award for *Happy Families* in 1960.

Taylor himself was awarded a Guggenheim Memorial Fellowship for 1950–51 and a grant from the National Institute of Arts and Letters in 1952. Under a Fulbright grant in 1956, he was able to do research in Paris for a projected (but later abandoned) play on Confederate statesmen and other Southerners who settled in Paris after the Civil War. With a Ford Foundation Fellowship in 1961 he was able to spend a year at the Royal Court Theatre in London studying theater techniques. A Rockefeller Foundation grant in 1965 and a senior fellowship from the National Endowment for the Arts in 1984 were both welcome support for his writing. Taylor was inducted into the National Institute of Arts and Letters in 1969, which in turn voted him into the highly selective and prestigious American Academy of Arts and Letters in 1983; he received the Gold Medal for the short story from both groups in 1978.

Only during the last few years, however, have the kind of honors the public really notices come to Taylor. The PEN/Faulkner Award for fiction to *The Old Forest* in 1986 was the first of these, followed by both the Ritz Hemingway Prize for fiction and the Pulitzer Prize for *A Summons to Memphis* in 1987. Taylor was also being considered for the American Book Award in 1986 until he dramatically withdrew his name from consideration in protest over a literary contest that declares losers as well as winners. Though Taylor no doubt must be pleased that the belated recognition has increased his readership and kept most of his books available in paperback reprints, he remains basically nonchalant about a sort of acclaim he doesn't "require." "If I wanted to make my fortune," he told one interviewer, "I'd have gone into the real estate business."[23]

The world of letters is lucky that Peter Taylor chose instead to speculate in the territory of the human heart, where he has staked his claim to some formidable themes. The discordant effects of time and change, the home and family as cultural microcosm, the sorrow of alienation and betrayal, the yearning for missed experience, the burden of history, tradition, and noblesse oblige—these are just a few of the mysteries that he explores first from one position and then from another. "I don't know the answer to anything, in a way, and yet I'm eternally interested in these questions," he says simply. "You create stories by weighting it one way so that this will seem to be true, and then another time, the other. To me this is what life is more like than working out a big system."[24]

Collectively, though, the works of Peter Taylor, just by asking and reasking the right questions, keep us in touch with the meanings and values that give significance to the human journey through life. As Taylor takes and retakes the measure of his world, he helps each of us take the measure of our individual worlds as well.

Chapter Two

A Long Fourth

"The Old Ways and the Old Teachings"

"The Scoutmaster," the first story in Peter Taylor's initial volume, *A Long Fourth,*[1] epitomizes in many ways the themes and techniques that dominate Taylor's early stories and remain influential in the work of his later career. It not only introduces his favorite subject matter of urban Southern upper-middle-class domestic life and his favorite narrative method of the conversational digressive-reflective family chronicle, but it also dramatizes basic insights about time, change, and cultural roles that receive frequent corroboration in his other works.

An awareness of time is present in "The Scoutmaster" from the first word to the last. The first-person narrator harkens back to the central events of the story—events that took place when he was about ten years old—from an adult position that gives perspective to these long-ago incidents. "That year all the young people in Nashville were saying, 'Don't tell me that, old dear, because it makes me *too* unhappy,'" the story begins, locating the action in a specific temporal context. But the time of the story is not just "that year," probably in the late 1920s, in which certain incidents occurred. It is also the unspecified present from which the past is being viewed. Further, it is the more remote past of historical record, the times through which the narrator's father and uncles have lived, for instance, and of romantic legend, what Uncle Jake refers to as "the golden days when a race of noble gentlemen and gracious ladies inhabited the land of the South." And it is, finally, the durative contour of time in which discrete units of the calendar are indistinguishable.

Philosophically, time may be described as a concept forced on human consciousness by the evidence of change—by the operation of the principle of mutability in the environment. And it is thus that time impinges on the consciousness of the characters in "The Scoutmaster," for change is evident all about them. Some of the changes, though trivial in themselves, are disturbing to the characters as symptomatic of much larger changes that they sense but cannot name. The father, for instance, cannot "abide" the slang his teenage daughter Virginia Ann uses; the mother complains of Virginia Ann's too "liberal" use of makeup.

If ephemeral fads are hard to tolerate, the more permanent changes that time brings are even harder to accept. Uncle Jake, for one, has never fully adjusted to the deaths of his parents, of his brother Louis, or of his wife and daughter. "If only Margaret, herself, had lived to make him and Presh a home, he might not have forever been looking to the past," the narrator's father says, adding: "He might have taken hold of himself." Other changes, not so irrevocable as death, are nevertheless disconcerting in their own ways. The family finds it difficult to accept relatives' changes in religion, occupation, or marital status. Even the developing emotions of a child or adolescent can cause family upsets, as when Virginia Ann surprises Uncle Jake by responding with hurt feelings to his playful teasing about a boyfriend or when the young narrator reacts "in a beastly rage" to a practical joke by Uncle Jake.

The most crucial changes, however, are not so much those that involve physical circumstances as those that involve moral values. Such changes are often of culturewide occurrence, but they are most frequently recognized only as they are manifested in individuals. The central incident of "The Scoutmaster" is a dramatization of this kind of change and its effects on the family circle. The recognition of a baleful change occurs when the adult members of the family, returning home early from a rainy Thanksgiving Day football game, discover that Virginia Ann and her date had never even left for the game, but had remained at home, where they are found together on the living-room sofa. The boyfriend is driven from the house, Virginia Ann is banished to her room, and the entire family is plunged into shock and despondency.

The tense situation is keenly felt but only vaguely understood by the preadolescent narrator, who, as the only potential chaperone left at home in the absence of his parents, has been a kind of unwitting and unwilling accomplice to his sister's indiscretion. The boy can only take his cues from the older members of the family: from Brother, who confides disturbedly, "Well, they were only necking, but they sure were *at* it"; from Mother and Father, who try to distract themselves with cards and conversation; and finally from Uncle Jake, who makes an impromptu but heartfelt speech at a Boy Scout meeting later that evening.

From this episode the narrator learns something of the relationship between changes in cultural values and the roles people play in their daily lives. He already has an awareness that certain members of the family fill fairly clearly defined roles. "I would have said my mother's function was Motherhood and my father's Fatherhood," he notes at one point, only to learn later from his mother how much more complex the process of change now makes their roles.

In the course of the story, too, the narrator comes to recognize that the divorced aunt who brought her gaiety into their house for a short sojourn also filled a role. When Aunt Grace makes her departure, the young nephew senses a new truth, while gazing in "breathtaking amazement" at her appearance:

> I felt myself growing timid in her presence, for she had become a stranger to me . . . . And all those things that indicated that Aunt Grace was one sort of person now indicated that she was quite another sort. She was not the utterly useless if wonderfully ornamental member of the family. In the solid blueness of her eyes I was surely on the verge of finding some marvelous function for her personality . . . . I was about to find the reason why there should be one member of a boy's family who was wise or old-fashioned enough to sit with Mother and Father and discuss the things they could not abide in Virginia Ann and yet who was foolish or newfangled enough to enjoy the very things that Virginia Ann called "the last word." (*LF*, 7–8)[2]

More mysterious to the narrator is the role to be attributed to Uncle Jake, the gentle widower whose wistful nostalgia suffuses the household. Jake has none of Aunt Grace's newfangledness; he remains essentially "old-fashioned." The narrator's father articulates a truth about Jake that the narrator will discover for himself at the climax of the story: "He's really incapable of being very realistic about his dealing with people. His real calling, his real profession is, you know, that of the Scoutmaster. It's during those Thursday night meetings with the boys that poor Jake fulfills himself."

The Joycean epiphany that confirms this truth for the narrator comes at the scout meeting the night of Virginia Ann's disgrace. Brought along to the meeting so that he will be removed from the tense family situation for a while, the young narrator watches the unfamiliar ritualistic activity of the scout meeting transform the familiar friends of his brother into "total strangers." He feels "a kind of elevation" as he hears the list of adjectives—"loyal, brave, trustworthy, clean, reverent"—recited in the scout oath. Then, gradually, Uncle Jake, "losing himself in the role of the eternal Scoutmaster," becomes a "stranger," too.

> I realized now that Father had been right. This was Uncle Jake fulfilling himself. And to fulfill one's self was to remove one's self somehow beyond the reach of my own understanding and affection. It seemed that the known Uncle Jake had moved out of his body just as Aunt Grace had moved out of hers when she sang and laughed and as the Mother and Father whose hands I liked to have placed gently on the top of

my head left their bodies whenever they excluded all the world from their conversation. (*LF,* 30; *OF,* 294)

The exclusion of all the world is the inevitable concomitant of all role-playing, the narrator at last understands; and, when Uncle Jake, "the last human soul" to whom he might "turn" in a person-to-person relationship, becomes a "stranger" playing a "role," he feels himself "deserted." But this sense of alienation that grabs the child, as bit by bit he comes to adopt the adult habit of identifying individuals as roles instead of as persons, is only part of the revelation of this story. In addition, "The Scoutmaster" discriminates the special quality of the role that Jake has been destined to play.

This priest-prophet role, symbolized by the scoutmaster's functions of conducting rituals and of sermonizing in support of traditional values, is something "more serious" than the artist-clown "laughter and song" role of Aunt Grace and "more relentless" even than the parent-spouse education and ministration role of the mother and father. "Half ridiculous and half frightening" in his scout uniform, Uncle Jake performs with deadly solemnity the haruspical task that the mysterious changes of time perennially call for:

> In that cold, bare, bright room he was saying that it was our great misfortune to have been born in these latter days when the morals and manners of the country had been corrupted, born in a time when we could see upon the members of our own families—upon our own sisters and brothers and uncles and aunts—the effects of our failure to cling to the teachings and ways of our forefathers. And he was saying that it was our duty and great privilege, as Boy Scouts, to preserve those honorable things which were left from the golden days when a race of noble gentlemen and gracious ladies inhabited the land of the South. He was saying that we must preserve them until one day we might stand with young men from all over the nation to demand a return to the old ways and the old teachings everywhere. (*LF,* 30–31; *OF,* 295)

The old ways and the old teachings—these are to some degree the subject of all the remaining stories in *A Long Fourth.* Taylor asks many questions about his cultural heritage as a Southerner. Which of the traditional values matter most? How are they affected by time and change? What allegiance is owed to them? How are they to be evaluated against present conditions?

Characteristically, Taylor presents these problems as they confront the evolving consciousness of a child or a young adult approaching a new level of maturity. As in James Joyce, the youthful protagonist comes to terms with his beliefs and values by a series of epiphanies through which something of their essential significance is made manifest. In Peter Taylor, however, the resolution the protagonist typically reaches is not rejection of, or flight from, tradition, but some sort of adjustment of present experience to the legacy of the past.

"The Changed View from the Window"

Two stories of Taylor's first volume, "Sky Line" and "A Spinster's Tale," take up the reactions of sensitive children to the disturbing threats that time's changes pose to their domestic security. Written in 1939 and 1938, respectively, these two stories, the earliest pieces included in *A Long Fourth,* reveal the longtime concern Taylor has had for this theme. "Sky Line," the less artificial of the two stories (both of which are marked by self-conscious literary techniques), is especially Joycean in form—provoking comparisons to the famous opening montages of *A Portrait of the Artist as a Young Man.* The story is a series of fifteen chronological sections detailing important impressions of Jimmy, the boy protagonist, as he passes from the innocent wonderment of childhood to the world-weary resignation of a precocious adulthood. Besides the presence of Jimmy, the episodes are linked by several symbols emphasizing the changes of time.

The first of these symbols is the swaying vine-baskets that the boy's grandmother had hung on the porch. "Is it God knocking?" Jimmy asks in the first line of the story as he hears the wind blowing the baskets against the house. "No, no. That isn't God. That isn't God," an adult, probably his mother, answers him. This answer, however, is ironic; for, in the total context of the story, the answer should be, "Yes. That is God. That is the hand of the Prime Mover heard signalling the passage of time."

Like everything else that bombards the senses of the developing child, the swinging wire baskets leave their indelible mark on the consciousness—a mark graphically suggested by the chipped-off paint on the clapboard siding of the porch against which the baskets knocked for many years. Even after the grandmother is dead, the baskets removed, and the house repainted, Jimmy does not forget the clattering of the baskets, which he will ever associate with his grandmother and with the primeval innocence of that period of his childhood before the religious mystery of death intruded; the "sunken places" beneath the new paint remain to remind him "ever after" of those years.

A second key symbol is the one singled out for emphasis in the title: the changing skyline of the boy's neighborhood. In the days of the swinging baskets the suburb is largely undeveloped. But, where once there were only Jimmy's house, the house on the corner, and the speckled stucco house next door where a little girl lived, soon there are new houses "scattered along the winding streets and along his own block." The colored "For Sale" signs disappear as a new Catholic church with a yellow brick tower and a new public school building go up in vacant lots where the high yellow grass once looked to the boy like "the central plains of Africa." Later on there is a new drugstore on a nearby corner, and later still tall apartment houses appear on the horizon.

All the new buildings are the irrefutable evidence of change for the boy; even when he sometimes feels that something isn't "completely changed," he is kept away from it by another feeling that it "isn't as it has been." Strangely, it is not so much the effect of change as the process itself that disturbs him: "Things have changed in the suburb; repeatedly he has told the new children how things once were, he is that conscious of it; but something forever keeps him from trying to observe too closely just how the new buildings go up." And, despite the burgeoning skyline, Jimmy is ever mindful of prior states, content to think of "other wallpapers that he remembers" in a room or pleased to reflect "that under the paint the marks that the vine-baskets made are actually still there."

Also symbolic are the erosive forces of nature, the wind and especially the rain. The yellow light that precedes or follows a change in weather generally accompanies the major discoveries of the story. After the grandmother's funeral, for instance, "everything outside the living room window looks yellowish" and the "rain comes like a burst of tears." When the rivalry of the boy's father and the little girl's father manifests itself in a vicious game of catch one day, dark clouds gather until the afternoon light turns yellow and rain streams down like a waterfall. It is in the rain that the boy, a little older, catches the illness that gives him the delirious dream of his father and the little girl's mother "dead on the streetcar tracks"; and it is in the rain that, grown older still, he discovers the true relationship between his now-widowed father and the little girl's mother and visualizes "the dark scene on his mother's guest room bed." And, in the final scene of the story, the light of the afternoon is described as "yellow," even "bilious," when the boy learns of his father's marriage to the little girl's mother, right before "rain bursts upon him" and drives him to the final epiphany in the room of the little girl.

The dominant image of the story is the house itself, the center of the boy's growth and development. Apparently belonging to the grandmother in the days of the undeveloped skyline and passed on to the boy's mother who must struggle to keep it during the hard days of the Great Depression, it is finally inherited by the boy himself, to whom the house clearly represents the security of the past threatened by forces from within and without. Through its windows Jim sees the changes take place around him. Two such scenes are especially relevant. In the first, Jim, secure behind the black wire screen in his upstairs room, watches the little neighbor girl bobbing up and down in the round zinnia bed below on the day of her father's funeral. In the second scene the positions of the two are reversed: the girl is behind the screen of the upstairs window in what is now her own room, and Jim is down below in the zinnia bed. But, in the interval between the two scenes, much has happened: the little girl and her mother have auctioned off their furniture and moved in with Jim's family, Jim's father has lost his job and the little girl's mother has gone to work, Jim himself has been seriously ill and his mother has died, Jim has been moved into his father's room and the now-adolescent girl moved into his, Jim's father and the girl's mother have become first business associates, then lovers, and now husband and wife. Most significantly of all, as Jim's security has decreased and the little girl's increased, Jim has overtaken her in worldly understanding so that the girl, though older, seems to have "the innocence of someone years younger than himself, the innocence of a very little girl."

The final scene is charged with conflict, as pubescent sexuality brings the boy and girl together in the house deserted by their honeymooning parents. The boy has watched the encroachments of the girl and her mother into his family circle, and he has seen his father and his mother each made into a "different person" by their acceptance of this outside force. Now, as he stands bare-chested and wet with rain before the sluttish girl wiggling seductively in her negligee, he must decide whether he too will finally succumb:

> The rain falls outside the open window, and now and again a raindrop splashes through the screen onto his face. At last it is almost night when the rain stops, and if there is any unnatural hue in the light, it is green. His heart has stopped pounding now, and all the heat has gone from his face. He has heard the hanging baskets beat against the house and felt the silence after their removal. He has heard the baseball smacking in the wet gloves of the men and seen the furniture auctioned on the lawn. The end of his grandmother, the defeat of his mother, the despair of his father, and the resignation of his new stepmother are all in his mind. The remarkable thing in the changed view from the window which had once been his lies in the tall apartment houses which punctuate the horizon and in the boxlike, flat-roofed ones in his own neighborhood. Through this window the girl too, he knows, must have beheld changes. (*LF,* 106)[3]

His decision, however, emerges from these thoughts; and, when he turns back to the girl, it is evident that he will not capitulate. Although all is quietly understated here, the theme is clear: change cannot be escaped, but it need not be embraced.

"The Beastly Vision"

Unlike "Sky Line," "A Spinster's Tale" covers a period of only a few months; but it too is a story of disturbing change and marks a passage from childhood to adulthood. The protagonist is a young girl, just entering her teens, who faces change in a form more frightening and grotesque than the subtle and insinuating form that the boy faced in "Sky Line." "A Spinster's Tale," as the title suggests, is a first-person narrative, the retrospective account of the young girl now turned spinster. The action runs from October to May in an unspecified year, presumably around the turn of the century, in Nashville. The setting is again a family home—this time an old-fashioned, "shadowy," and "brutally elegant" town house with stained-glass windows, mosaic hearth, full-length mirror panels by the windows, beaded lampshades, cavernous hallways, red-carpeted stairways, and grandfather clocks.

The tale begins on a day, only a few months after her mother's death, when Elizabeth is still an innocent fairy-tale child, idly trying out chairs in the parlor like Goldilocks or peering in mirrors "trying to discover a resemblance between [herself] and the wondrous Alice who walked through a looking-glass." It is just as she is saying the magic wish-words "Away, away" to herself in the mirror that her vision slips from the mirror to the window and to the terrifying sight of the neighborhood drunkard, Mr. Speed, "walking like a cripple with one foot on the curb and one in the street."

What is there about the drunken old man that makes Elizabeth "dry-eyed" with fright? Numerous clues throughout the story suggest that Mr. Speed is the dreamlike projection of some unbridled masculine principle that the motherless girl unconsciously fears and resents. Elizabeth mentally associates Mr. Speed with the other males who surround her: with her eighteen-year-old brother, whose teenage carousing inspires puritanical predictions of eternal damnation; with her father and uncles, whose toddy drinking in the parlor produces a merry camaraderie the girl cannot broach; and with the young Benton boys (friends of her brothers), whose horseless carriage seems an invitation to wild adventure.

Elizabeth is aware of these links herself. The opening sentence of her story is a comparison of her fear *for* her brother with her fear *of* Mr. Speed, and later she puts into words the thought that in her brother and father she saw "something of Mr. Speed." Significantly, she adds: "And I knew that it was more than a taste for whisky they had in common." Later, she observes something in her brother's and her father's "nature" that was "fully in sympathy with the very brutality" of Mr. Speed's drunkenness. Her reactions to various happenings make it clear that a domineering male sexuality is a principal basis for this identification. Thus, the scene in which Elizabeth detains and beguiles her drunken brother in her bedroom is a preparation for the scene of her final confrontation with Mr. Speed, the action of which it helps to motivate. For Elizabeth will not allow herself to reflect too long about her "feelings" for her brother ("my desire for him to strike me and my delight in his natural odor") —feelings that derive from her own burgeoning adolescence and her unguided attempts to establish her own sexual identity.

That Elizabeth's attitude toward Mr. Speed is affected by her sexual feelings is also revealed by her thoughts the very first time she spies him, when she has a "sudden inexplicable memory" of her mother on her deathbed, apparently the victim of complications from the delivery of a stillborn baby. Though Elizabeth dwells only on the pleasant aspects of the memory (the warmth of her mother's cheek against hers) and represses the unpleasant (the mother suddenly sending her from the room and beckoning the nurse), the inference seems inevitable that she associates Mr. Speed subconsciously with the cause of her mother's death: with the male principle to which her mother submitted in pregnancy.

Furthermore, Elizabeth resents the "blustering tones of merry tolerance" with which her father and her uncles indulgently refer to Mr. Speed's drunken antics and the vulgar disdain with which her father refuses to hear of her fear of Mr. Speed. Her father, in fact, after giving her some sententious advice becomes in her eyes a kind of Mr. Speed himself: "He punched at his left side several times, gave a prolonged belch, settled a pillow behind his head, and soon was sprawled beside me on the settee, snoring." Elizabeth also thinks of Mr. Speed at other significant times. Hearing her father talk about hundreds of soldiers in the Union Depot before the Spanish-American War, she visualizes "all those men there, that close together" and finds it "something like meeting Mr. Speed in the front hall." And even a mental image of all the "pitiable" little girls in Miss Hood and Miss Herron's Belmont School "being called for by gentle ladies or by warm-breasted Negro women" conjures up "the beastly vision of Mr. Speed." Finally, there is her association of Mr. Speed with a primordial symbol of virile power—a wild horse. The horse image first comes up when Elizabeth's brother tries to frighten her with a pointless anecdote: "I saw three horses running away out on Harding Road today! . . . They were running to beat hell and with little girls riding them!" It occurs again in the last line of the story when the Elizabeth of the present, commenting on her recurring memories of the Mr. Speed episode, notes that

"It was only the other night that I dreamed I was a little girl on Church Street again and that there was a drunk horse in our yard." The significance of the image is made explicit, however, when Elizabeth comments to her brother:

> "I wouldn't mind him less if he were sober," I said. "Mr. Speed's like—a loose horse."
> This analogy convinced him. He knew then what I meant.
> "You mustn't waste your time being afraid of such things," he said in great earnestness. "In two or three years there'll be things that you'll have to be afraid of. Things you really can't avoid." (*LF,* 118; *ML,* 178)[4]

Not only does this passage point to Mr. Speed's oneiric meaning, it also points to the underlying cause of the girl's anxieties: the changes that adolescence is bringing to her life. The situation becomes transparent in the dream Elizabeth has about a "little girl whose hands began to get very large." "Grown men came for miles around to look at the giant hands and to shake them," Elizabeth recounts; "but the little girl was ashamed of them and hid them under her skirt." At first, in the dream, Elizabeth is an onlooker who laughs uproariously at the little girl's fear; then she becomes the little girl. The recollection of the dream is juxtaposed with a recollection of the birthday when Elizabeth's father gives her a dressing table with the inscription "For my young lady daughter." That is the same day that Elizabeth begins to put up her hair, adult-fashion, in a knot on the back of her head.

Aware of her own maturation, Elizabeth has "an intuitive knowledge" that Mr. Speed is "a permanent and formidable figure" in her life which she will "be called upon to deal with." Eventually, she comes to accept his existence "as a natural part" of her life, though "something to be guarded against" or "to be thoroughly prepared for" when it comes. By the time Mr. Speed does arrive at her door, Elizabeth has "done everything that a little girl, now fourteen, could do in preparation for such an eventuality," including taking her place as mistress in the motherless household. She experiences for the last time "the inconsolable desperation of childhood" at the moment that the drunken old man staggers through the rain to her porch. Then, though one part of her longs to hide her face in a lost maternal bosom, another part of her makes her "deal with Mr. Speed, however wrongly."

The "dealing with" Mr. Speed is the denouement of the story. While the old reprobate petrifies the black maid with his phallic cane and his brutal oaths, Elizabeth acts out her inevitable role "with courage but without wisdom" and summons the police in the Black Maria to come get him. "I saw myself as a little beast adding to the injury that what was bestial in man had already done him," Elizabeth admits, adding: "I was frightened by the thought of the cruelty which I found I was capable of, a cruelty which seemed inextricably mixed with what I had called courage."

Despite this insight, Elizabeth's decisive action at this point has already set the pattern for her whole life. By rejecting Mr. Speed and refusing to minister to him when, knocked unconscious by a fall on the steps, he lies helpless before her in the beating rain, she rejects the uxorial and maternal role of womanhood and symbolically elects her spinsterhood. Like Mr. Speed's own old-maid sister, Elizabeth feels ever bound to him: "My hatred and fear of what he stood for in my eyes has never left me. And since the day that I watched myself say 'away' in the mirror, not a week has passed but that he has been brought to my mind by one thing or another." The title of the story confirms the reader's predictions for her future: unlike the protagonist of "Sky Line" who learns to cope successfully with the anxieties induced by time's changes, the unfortunate girl of "A Spinster's Tale," arresting her own development, withdraws into a solitary role where the speedy changes of life's cycles can no longer affect her.

"The Sum of a Thousand Accidents"

Though time's changes are perhaps most evident to children, the problems that the passage of time creates are not limited to those of growing up. Two of Peter Taylor's stories in *A Long Fourth,* "Allegiance" and "Rain in the Heart," dramatize problems all people have when they attempt to evaluate new experience against norms drawn from the past. It is probably not coincidental that both of these stories are set in World War II—a period of violent change naturally conducive to the reassessment of traditional values.

In "Allegiance" a young soldier from Nashville is brought by the exigencies of wartime into a situation he would probably never otherwise have faced—a situation where he must examine in person the subject of a family myth, a myth he had always previously taken at face value. The scene is London, far from the parochial atmosphere of his familiar environment and from the dominating influence of his mother's point of view. For this young man has, up to the moments recounted in the story, habitually accepted without question his mother's version of an incident in the past that led to the estrangement of his mother and her older sister, the young man's aunt. He has indeed a "heritage of resentment" against his elegant aunt, whom he believes to have "grievously wronged" his mother "in a manner so subtle and base" that he has never known or even wished to know its nature. He has, moreover, a "silent pact" with his now-dead mother that forbids him even to hear the other side of the case as he might if he were to open his aunt's letters. He has in short an "allegiance" that he does not intend to betray.

The story opens, however, with the words "Come in," spoken by the aunt—words that are on one level a mere polite invitation to enter the aunt's apartment, but on another a summons to enter into another point of view. The young man is amazed that his aunt can "dare to presume" his acceptance of her bid, yet he acquiesces, albeit "with trepidation," afraid that he will "yield" more than he wishes. The imagery suggests the archetypal encounter of the quest hero and the legendary enchantress. The aunt acknowledges to her soldier nephew, "You want only to accomplish your mission and get yourself home again," yet she is clearly concerned to win him over to herself. She is described as "still a great beauty," a woman of "charm" and "fascination" (her "romantic quality"), possessed of "a sort of mystical, superhuman ignorance" of her own activities but capable of enduring anything "to gain her ends." "I feel that I am in the presence of some newfangled sort of idolater and conjurer," the young man says as he listens to his aunt draw on her ageless memory to cast a spell of words by which she makes herself and her exotic den of a room seem to "constitute the only certainty." There is in her attitude the hint of "some magic potency to the mere actuality of the moment" and "to the sound of her own voice," and the nephew feels "a sort of literal enchantment . . . where all the past and all the future and all occurrences of the exterior world are of no consequence."

In such circumstances, it is no wonder that the young man feels that he may at some point "betray someone or something." As the interview proceeds, the "uncertainties" of his mind increase; and he becomes unsure whether his consciousness of betrayal is of "a possibility or a fact." His guilty fear is crystallized in the moment when his eyes and those of the aunt meet for an instant in the mirror, and he hears the sound of their "commingled" laughter.

But what is it that is so subject to betrayal? As in so many other Peter Taylor stories, time is the issue at question. The soldier has inherited from his mother not just her version of some past injury from the aunt, but her vision of time as well—a vision that underlies her interpretation of the past injury. Although the mother's view is nowhere articulated in the story, it can be inferred as the opposite of the aunt's view of time, a view that the young man explicitly discusses. His aunt, the nephew discerns, has a "concern only for what is actual," and she has a "faith in the actual's being but the sum of a thousand accidents." Thus to her mind, interpersonal relationships (such as the past one between herself and her sister and the present one between herself and the young man) are the result of fortuitous compilations of circumstances rather than human volition. As the nephew understands her, she feels no responsibility for the past and no undue anxiety for the present, only a reliance on the happy arrangement of accidents.

Contrasted with this view is the history-burdened view of the mother, who found nothing accidental in the past event that estranged the sisters. From the young man's attitude toward the aunt, we can sense his inherited belief in human choice as the efficient cause of good and evil; he is both shocked and fascinated by the aunt's faith in accidents, and he longs to disprove the "worth" of that faith. Ironically, it is his own beliefs, not hers, that are brought into doubt, that are, in fact, almost betrayed in the charmed presence of his "complicated and worldly" aunt.

When the young narrator leaves the aunt's apartment, he is still awestruck by the "fate" he might have met before the aunt's "absolute authority." He has escaped, somehow, the enchantress's final spell, but he has not escaped to freedom. Even though his mind remains "troubled by a doubt of the reality of all things" and "haunted for a while by an unthinkable distrust for the logic and rarefied judgments" of his dead mother, he feels himself "still a prisoner in her parlor in Nashville." His allegiance to the norm of the past, represented by his mother, is too deep-rooted to be dispelled even by the magic fascination of his foreign adventure.

The hero of "Rain in the Heart" is also a young soldier from Tennessee who is brought into a position where he must reassess his traditional values. Both setting and situation are far more ordinary in this story, however, and the hero faces no antagonist so formidable as the aunt in "Allegiance." This soldier is a drill sergeant, stationed at a Southern army post (apparently Fort Oglethorpe, Georgia, just a few miles from Chattanooga, Tennessee), who has an overnight pass to permit him to visit his recent bride for the first time since their honeymoon. En route from drill field to barracks to bus to streetcar to furnished apartment, he has several encounters that lead him to a moment of deep reflectiveness about the "terrible unrelated diversity in things."

The sergeant is characterized at once as one who cherishes traditional values: home, family, romantic love, the good life, the beauty of nature, the heritage from the past. Even as he sets out on his journey to his bride, he carries with him a symbolic burden—"a big volume of Civil War history" from the city library. This "heavy, dark history book" puts into perspective for him not only the present war for which he is drilling rookies, but also other aspects of modern life. He is acutely aware, for instance, that the ridge where his bride has found an apartment is the site of a bloody Civil War battle—presumably, though it is not mentioned by name, the Battle of Chickamauga, where over sixteen thousand on each side were killed. He is sure, moreover, that if he had lived at the time of the battle he "would have seen ever so clearly the Cause for that fighting."

On his way he picks up another symbolic item, a bouquet of sweet peas given him by a peculiar cleaning woman whom he meets at a streetcar stop. Unlike the cleaning woman who professes to hate the nonutilitarian flowers, the sergeant can appreciate them for their aesthetic and romantic value, and he gives them to his wife who arranges them in a vase. The flowers become at the climax of the story the catalyst that sets off the sergeant's speculative mood, the rain in his heart. The bride herself is, of course, the chief symbol of the values the drill sergeant has been taught to love and respect. At the camp, the sergeant wistfully recalls the image of "her soft, Southern voice, her small hands forever clasping a handkerchief"; but, when he actually sees her again, he finds her voice softer, her appearance fairer than he had remembered. Between them there is "complete understanding and sympathy," so much so that her qualities are brought to mind even when the sergeant sees his own face in the mirror.

The "old-fashioned" apartment that the bride has found is a retreat from the vulgar world of the army camp. Riding toward it on the bus, the sergeant recognizes that where he once perceived "a genteel suburban life" as "intolerable by its restrictions and confinements," he now dreams longingly "of the warm companionship he would find with her and their sober neighbors in a house with a fine roof." The vulgarity, amorality, and rootlessness of the other soldiers at the barracks contrast with the taste, order, and decorum represented by his bride and their apartment: "How unreal to him were these soldiers and their hairy bodies and all their talk and their rough ways. How temporary. How different from his own life, from his real life with her." Similarly, the bitter, ugly, puritanlike repression of sex and sensuality he discerns in the cleaning woman seems at the other extreme from his connubial bliss.

All of these things—symbols of traditional values and of their opposites—bring the sergeant to a point of philosophical realization as he lies in bed beside his young wife. He has been thinking of the Civil War battle once fought in this area, of the sweet peas his wife has placed in a vase, and of his wife's perception and understanding; but his thoughts are interrupted by a rumbling streetcar.

> And before he could even speak the thoughts which he had been thinking, all those things no longer seemed to matter. The noise of the street car, the irregular rumble and uncertain clanging, brought back to him once more all the incidents of the day. He and his wife were here beside each other, but suddenly he was hopelessly distracted by this new sensation. The street car had moved away now beyond his hear-

ing, and he could visualize it casting its diffused light among the dark foliage and over the white gravel between the tracks. He was left with the sense that no moment in his life had any relation to another. It was as though he were living a thousand lives. And the happiness and completeness of his marriage could not seem so large a thing. (*LF,* 86–87; *OF,* 254–55)

He is, in fact, able to clasp his bride in his arms again only when the rain begins once more outside: the rain that has made them seem "even more alone" in their newlyweds' apartment, the rain that sets them off like the "pleasing isolated arrangement of objects" his bride had made on the table in the living room.

"The Fancy Woman"

It is appropriate that the sergeant in "Rain in the Heart" should come to reckon with his values when he leaves the all-male world of the army camp and travels to his bride's apartment. Peter Taylor has always been fascinated with the mythic roles that cultures thrust upon women, and throughout his career, but most especially in his early stories, he has delighted in probing the impact such mythic expectations can have on individual women. A final pair of stories in his first volume provides a contrast between two principal female archetypes: woman as Lilith, the destructive principle, in "The Fancy Woman," and woman as Eve, the tutelary spirit who presides over and protects cultural values, in "A Long Fourth."

"The Fancy Woman," one of the most frequently anthologized and consequently one of the best known of Taylor's stories, is in characterizations and point of view a very untypical sample of his work. Written while Taylor was still a Kenyon student in response to a taunt by Robert Lowell that Taylor was "prim and puritanical" and "didn't know anything about the world," it was conceived as "a story about a woman who is so corrupt that she can't recognize innocence when she sees it"; Taylor wrote its provocative first sentence ("He wanted no more of her drunken palaver") with no idea of where he was going from there.[5]

The central character, who provides the point of view for the whole story, is the "fancy woman" of the title, a Memphis trollop temporarily uprooted and uncomfortably transplanted to the country estate of a wealthy lothario. During her brief pastoral adventure the tarnished nymph Josie feels herself alternately humiliated and petted by her erstwhile lover George, patronized and mocked by his servants and his guests from the city, and finally solicited and snubbed by his sons. Josie has an almost paranoid sensitivity to the opinions of the supercilious strangers she confronts, but she lacks the fervor to counter them effectively. The kind of person who sizes up all other persons in terms of contrast to herself, she is very much aware that she is white and the servants she believes to be spying on her are black, that she is youngish and the visitors' wives are aging, that she comes from one background and all these new people from another.

The most painful contrast is the one she senses between herself and George. Although he is clearly from a higher class, with more education, more money, more sense, but no more manners (deliberately insulting her, as he does, with tasteless language and decorum), Josie comes to see him as "no different from a floorwalker." Since it was a floorwalker who systematically degraded Josie in her last job at a department store, Josie is identifying George with the exploiting class—the kind who get a "hold" on others and use them dispassionately for their own ends, showing "no remorse, no compassion, and no humor." She decides to turn the tables by finding out what is wrong inside George ("for there's something wrong inside everybody") and getting a "hold" on him somehow:

> She had had her fill of him and everybody else and was going to look out for her own little sweet self from now on.
>
> That was her trouble, she knew. She'd never made a good thing of people. "That's why things are like they are now," she said. "I've never made a good thing out of anybody." But it was real lucky that she realized it now, just exactly when she had, for it was certain that there had never been one whom more could be made out of than George. (*LF,* 38; *ML,* 141–42; *CS,* 174)

Josie sees the chance she wants when unexpected visitors drive out from Memphis and she realizes that George, who had "scorned and laughed at everybody and every situation," will be ashamed of her before his guests: "On her behavior would depend his comfort. She was cold sober and would be *up* to whatever showed itself. It was her real opportunity."

Thinking she has the upper hand, Josie imagines herself "soaring" upward into "the beginning of a new life" in which she might become "one of them"—one of the neatly corseted matrons with "lovely profiles and soft skin and natural-colored hair," one of George's own kind. That dream is shattered, however, as Josie, tiptoeing down the stairs, hears George and his men friends engaged in bawdy banter about her. "The girls are gonna be decent to her," she hears them say. "They agreed in the yard." Hearing, too, that George's teenage sons are coming the next day, Josie feels that she is "descending . . . once more into her old world": "He'll slick me some way if he has to for his kids, I think."

Josie is not immediately aware that her prime opportunity lies with the sons, not with the society guests. After an evening of drunken dancing and none-too-subtle flirtation, Josie even winds up sleeping with one of the guests. This incident is a psychological turning point for Josie, complete with moral revelation:

> "They're none of 'em any better than the niggers. I knew they couldn't be. Nobody is. By God, nobody's better than I am. Nobody can say anything to me." Everyone would like to live as free as she did! There was no such thing as . . . There was no such thing as what the niggers and the whites liked to pretend they were. She was going to let up, and do things in secret. Try to look like an angel. It wouldn't be as hard since there was no such thing. (*LF,* 48; *ML,* 152–53; *CS,* 185–86)

The next day Josie meets George's sons—Jock, seventeen; Buddy, fourteen—who look "like two of those lovely wax models in the boy's department at Jobe's." Convinced now that even the supposedly innocent have smutty souls, Josie is humiliated when Buddy, reciting verses from Swinburne's "A Match" to the lady guests, chooses for her the one with the lines: "If you were queen of pleasure / And I were king of pain . . . ." Later, during the night, she suspects that one of the boys is even trying to enter her bedroom through a bath that adjoins their room and hers.

The situation is now ripe for a melodramatic denouement in which the poor mistreated strumpet can seduce the son and wreak revenge on her sadistic oppressor. Taylor has, indeed, skillfully suggested such a possibility. George's Achilles' heel has already been foreshadowed in the very first paragraph of the story in a casual allusion to the two half-grown sons he is "so mortally proud of," a phrase repeated at the point where Josie discovers one of the sons has "notions." Furthermore, George has been described as gazing at his boys "like a floorwalker charmed by his wax manikins which had come to life." When George sends the elder son back to town, but inadvertently leaves Buddy alone in the house with Josie, the sentimental climax seems inevitable.

Taylor is much too serious an artist, even in this very early story, to provide so facile a conclusion. When Buddy asks Josie, "Don't you think it's time you did something nice for me?" and requests her to pose for him, Josie assumes he means for her to pose in the nude as a preliminary to something further. But Taylor has Buddy unexpectedly reject Josie's inference: "'That's not what I mean,' she heard the kid say again, without blinking an eye, without blushing. 'I didn't know you were that sort of nasty thing here. I didn't believe you were a fancy woman. Go on out of here. Go away!' he ordered her." Josie, then, instead of triumphing over the hypocritical world around her the way romanticized demimondes traditionally do, descends the stairs once more in dejection. She is left to await the angry displeasure of George, "wondering what he'd do to her."

The conclusion of "The Fancy Woman" is thus right for the purpose of both realistic characterization and thematic development. From the first scene on, Josie has revealed herself as a weak, foolish, and irresolute woman who indulges in dream victories over enemies, real and imagined (witness her dream conquest of the black servant, Amelia, and her fantasy of becoming good friends with one of the society matrons), but who can never take the first step in executing any plan of action (for instance, giving up the liquor that is her frequent undoing). She is, indeed, a "fancy woman" in more than one sense, for she lives in a world of illusions.

The chief insight of the story is also dependent upon the antiromantic reversal at the end of the action. For Taylor does not believe Josie is right in her assumption that there is "no such thing" as the codes of values that others aspire to live by. Without any evidence beyond her own preconceptions, Josie has convinced herself that the black servants must be "all dosed up" because of promiscuity like her own, that the scar on Amelia's wrist must be a knife slash inflicted by the man-servant Henry ("who probably had raped his own children, the way niggers do"), that the cook Mammy steals food and has "likely killed enough niggers in her time to fill Jobe's basement." The same type of presuppositions apply to the white visitors, who she suspects will reveal their "true colors" and not act any better than she does "after they've got a few under their belts."

The damage Buddy does to her final hypothesis that "nobody's as damn smutty as a smart-alecky shaver" puts a new light on her basic judgment that "everyone would like to live as free as she did." It is not that Josie has necessarily misjudged everyone; there is positive proof that some she meets (the guest who winds up in bed with her, for instance) are no better than she pictures them. Taylor does not even rule out the possibility that Jock and Buddy did have the very "notions" Josie suspected. The point is simply that Buddy did reject Josie and that he did so on moral grounds. Though there are hypocrites enough in the world, just as Josie deems, the world is not totally hypocritical; freedom from values and moral codes is not the desired lot of *all* humankind.

Because she has not learned this truth, Josie, the "queen of pleasure," must be ever paired with the "king of pain," the sadist-lover who steps outside his own code to use the queen of pleasure and then contemptuously punishes her for her own amoral compliance. Without the moral values to support woman's hereditary role, Josie is an artificial substitute for what the traditional society expects women to be, and she herself cannot tell the real from the imitation. When Josie admires an old vine-filled bucket that seems to go with the brick cistern that forms the base of the quaint breakfast table, a black servant sets her straight in words that apply not just to the bucket but to Josie as well: "'No'm,' Amelia said . . . . 'They brung that out f'om Memphis and put it there like it was it.'"

"The Real Tennessee Version"

In the last story of his first volume, the story that gives the title to the book, Peter Taylor shows that the real and legitimate mistress of a house can have problems, too. Harriet Wilson of "A Long Fourth" becomes, in fact, the thematic opposite of Josie Carlson in "The Fancy Woman." As conventional as Josie is unconventional, Harriet, a plump and pretty matron just past fifty, has no desire for the freedom Josie delights in. Her life is ruled by maxims from three respected sources of authority upon which women of her type have traditionally relied: mother, husband, and adult son. If Harriet has any uneasiness in accepting the guidance of these authorities, it is only when the instruction of the first two, which gives her comfort, conflicts with the instruction of the last, which sometimes disturbs her.

Though brilliantly individuated and perhaps more fully realized than any other character in Taylor's first book, Harriet is quickly seen to have symbolic significance as a latter-day hearth goddess, a custodian of domestic virtues and values. Living in an "old-fashioned" house, tending in her housekeeping to rigidity and an overdone care for "cleanliness and order," maintaining an expert interest in matters of genealogy and kinship, holding romantic attachments to the home environment, and loving inordinately "the old songs that were fixed so well in her ear and in her heart," Harriet is almost the archetypal mother. Like the version of the ballad "Barbara Allen" that she sings, she is authentic—"the real Tennessee version" of what she stands for.

Harriet's firm grounding in a particular cultural reality limits her ability to recognize others as variants on the same maternal role. Specifically, she fails to see any parallel between herself and her old black servant Mattie or, later and less importantly, between herself and Ann Prewitt, the modern girl her son brings home on a visit.

Harriet goes into paroxysms of indignation when Mattie points out a similarity in their two situations. On this Fourth of July weekend in a year during World War II (presumably 1943), Harriet is awaiting a farewell visit from her son before he goes into the army, when Mattie learns that her nephew BT, whom she has raised as a foster son, must go to work at "th'air fact'ry" to avoid being drafted. "It's like you losin' Mr. Son," Mattie says of her own plight. Despite her patronizing affection for Mattie, Harriet is appalled—ostensibly by the suggested similarity between her own dear son and Mattie's odiferous nephew, but perhaps subconsciously by the identification of herself and Mattie in the same maternal role.

The details of the story suggest that the identification Mattie makes is more pertinent than Harriet realizes. Both Harriet and Mattie represent values their "sons" have repudiated. Son, despite his reputation as a "model son" who doesn't grieve his parents "with youthful dissipation as most Nashville boys do," nevertheless has "advanced ideas" that seem "peculiar" and "radical" to the people of Nashville and writes "disturbing articles" in national magazines. And BT, though "acknowledged a good hand at many services which could be rendered on the back porch" in the open air, lacks the qualities white people like Harriet find attractive in his Aunt Mattie and other blacks: "He had neither good manners nor the affectionate nature nor the appealing humor that so many niggers have." Neither Son nor BT follows the traditional moral codes of the era; the intellectual Son does not believe in marriage, and BT brings black "female-things" from Nashville to his shack. Furthermore, both are about to be lost to their "mothers" because of forces larger than the individuals involved—the distant but destructive war.

Son's holiday homecoming finally leads Harriet to a new self-awareness. The catalyst is found in Harriet's spitefully spinsterish daughters, Kate and Helena, who set out on a deliberate campaign to embarrass Son and his "Platonic" girl friend, Ann Prewitt, by aping cloyingly the qualities of Southern womanhood that Harriet takes seriously. When Harriet hears them mincing out "the very reverse of ideas they usually expressed" (including the etiquette of Harriet's mother and the philosophy of the Vanderbilt Agrarians) and pretending allegiance to "the customs and ways that used to pertain in Nashville," she is pleased—until she finally realizes they are maliciously parodying all that is conventional in her way of life.

Her shock is compounded when she learns that Son has apparently acted with the same sort of callous cruelty to his unconventional friend who has quite conventionally fallen in love with him. And Ann Prewitt, though she is the editor of a birth-control magazine and ostensibly an intellectual radical, is perhaps closer in her values to Harriet than any of Harriet's own children; she, at least, has an emotional center capable of sensitivity and love. "*Her* girls had never been in love," Harriet is made to realize at one point. "They're like Son . . . and it isn't in them."

Disappointed in her own maternal relationships (the hoped-for moment when Son would come to tell her "what is in his heart" never materializes), Harriet discovers that Mattie suffers too when BT brings one of his black "female-things" to the shack his last night home. Sweetheart, Harriet's husband, insists that Harriet go to comfort Mattie. Not understanding their estrangement, he asks, "Harriet, why should this be so hard for you?"—a question that Harriet feels is "making a larger and more general inquiry into her character" than had ever been done before. When Harriet does go and apologize to Mattie in BT's reeking shack, the scene is poignant:

> Mattie raised her eyes to her mistress, and there was neither forgiveness nor resentment in them. In her protruding lower lip and in her wide nostrils there was defiance, but it was a defiance of the general nature of this world where she must pass her days, not of Harriet in particular. In her eyes there was grief and there was something beyond grief. After a moment she did speak, and she told Harriet that she was going to sit here all night and that they had all better go on to bed in the house. Later when Harriet tried to recall the exact tone and words Mattie had used—as her acute ear would normally have allowed her to do—she could not reconstruct the speech at all. It seemed as though Mattie had used a special language common to both of them but one they had never before discovered and could now never recover. (*LF,* 165–66; *OF,* 235)

Back in her room, Harriet tries successively to resume her broken prayers, to weep, and to comprehend her experience: "it seemed that her children no longer existed; it was as though they had all died in childhood as people's children used to do." But her memory keeps returning to the image of Mattie waiting up in BT's shack.

The conflicts in "A Long Fourth," then, are not the apparent ones: the conflicts between generations with differing ideas or between races of different status. Harriet is not cut off from her children because they are radical and she is conservative and conventional, but because she holds some values and ideals, and they hold none. And the superficial estrangement, based on racial and social distinctions, between herself and Mattie is not a lasting one because the two women share something more fundamental in their common role of "mother."

Ann Prewitt has mentioned that Son has been reading Oswald Spengler's *Decline of the West,* and the allusion provides a clue to a possible interpretation of the story. The story's situation could almost be a microcosm set up to demonstrate Spengler's cultural theories. The living Southern "Culture" (preserving the fundamentals of the Western heritage) represented by

Harriet is being succeeded by the declining "Civilization" stage represented by Harriet's children, especially Son. Harriet, Mattie, and Ann are all variations on Spengler's concept of woman: standing close to the Cosmic, rooted deep in the earth, immediately "involved in the grand cyclic rhythms of Nature," actually being (rather than experiencing, making, or comprehending) Destiny, History, Time. For woman, Spengler says, history is a uniform "cosmic flow," whereas for man history is "political, social, more conscious, freer, and more agitated than the other." Spengler argues:

> Here, in man and in woman, *the two kinds of History* are fighting for power. Woman is strong and wholly what she is, and she experiences the Man and the Sons only in relation to herself and her ordained role. In the masculine being, on the contrary, there is a certain contradiction; he is the man, and he is something else besides, which woman neither understands nor admits, which she feels as robbery and violence upon that which to her is holiest . . . .
>
> And so woman despises that other History—man's politics—which she never comprehends, and of which all that she sees is that it takes her sons from her . . . . Man's history sacrifices woman's history to itself, . . . but nevertheless there was and is and ever will be a secret politic of the woman . . . that seeks to draw away her male from his kind of history and to weave his body and soul into her own plantlike history of generic succession—that is, unto herself . . . .
>
> Thus, history has two meanings, neither to be blasphemed. It is cosmic or politic, it *is* being or it *preserves* being . . . . The double significance of directional Time finds its highest expression in the ideas of *the State* and *the Family*.[6]

In Spengler's theory of the organic life cycle of cultures, fertility belongs to the Culture stage and sterility to the Civilization stage. "The primary woman . . . is *mother*," Spengler says; and Taylor has made Harriet a real mother and Mattie an equally committed foster mother. "But now emerges the Ibsen woman, the comrade, the heroine of a whole megalopolitan literature from Northern drama to Parisian novel," Spengler adds. "Instead of children, she has soul-conflicts; marriage is craft-art for the achievement of 'mutual understanding.'"[7] And Taylor gives us Ann Prewitt, the birth-control proponent, the Platonic mistress, the woman with soul-conflicts and no children.

Is Taylor arguing that Western culture, or at least its manifestation in the southern United States, has (to use Spengler's metaphor) passed its fecund summer? In the last line of the story Taylor writes: "When she opened her eyes it was dark and there was the chill of autumn night about the room." The inference is possible (especially when we recall that Harriet has just noted that her children seemed no longer to exist, to have died in childhood), but there is no compulsion to make it. Even without the Spenglerian analogies, "A Long

Fourth" is on its most literal level a subtle enough story about the complexities of cultural values—old and new, male and female, black and white. As the final story of a volume that began with "The Scoutmaster," its simple and sufficient point may be that the young men from all over the nation have not yet demanded—as Uncle Jake hoped they might someday—"a return to the old ways and the old teachings everywhere."

Chapter Three

A Woman of Means

A Slightly Larger Scale

Two years after his critically well-received debut with *A Long Fourth* Peter Taylor was negotiating with Harcourt, Brace about a manuscript that, at about thirty-five thousand words, was difficult to categorize. Taylor has recalled that though this was still a relatively long work for him, it "could have been much longer" if he had not (as was his wont) "thrown away as much as [he] finally kept." The publisher wasn't sure it could be published as a novel, Taylor threatened to withdraw it, and the publisher finally wrote back "saying he had decided to print it." "Perhaps he still didn't like it but thought I had other novels up my sleeve," Taylor has said.[1]

The resulting publication was *A Woman of Means* (1950),[2] marketed as a novel, but perhaps more accurately described as a novelette. With only a small cast of characters, a plot without a great deal of external drama, a carefully controlled tonal unity, and none of the flashy fireworks usually associated with commercial fiction, it was in a way only the magnification of Taylor's short-story methods to a slightly larger scale.

As might be expected from the stories that preceded it, *A Woman of Means* is another retrospective first-person narrative about urban family life. Specifically, it is an account of an adolescent boy's complex relationship with a wealthy and doting stepmother and of the stepmother's neurotic disintegration. The narrator is Quintus Cincinnatus Lovell Dudley, whose unfashionable name, as a reflection of his Tennessee heritage, is one key to the role he plays. Quint is a half-orphan whose mother died at his birth and left him to be reared by his father alone. But Quint's father, Gerald Dudley, is a traveling hardware salesman, and being raised by him meant moving from boardinghouse to boardinghouse and transferring from school to school in town after town. Still, Quint has a close camaraderie with his father and accepts his vision "that in a few years he and I would *have things* and *be somebody* ourselves."

During the summers Quint was usually sent to Belgrove, his maternal grandmother's farm in Tennessee. Grandma Lovell's place is, from one point of view, "a run-down farm" belonging to "a poor-little-old country woman," as Quint's father sometimes describes it. But it also has romantic souvenirs of another day: a lone white oak and a solitary magnolia, an old, abandoned, formal garden with broken urns and untrimmed hedges, a cannon on the lawn and a stack of rusty shells on the ell porch, the grass-covered mounds of an Indian graveyard, and nearby trenches where Confederate soldiers had died in the Battle of Nashville.

Quint's rural pursuits are severely limited, however, by the overprotective restrictions his father makes and insists Grandma Lovell must enforce. Gerald Dudley will not let his son go barefooted for more than a minute, will not let him venture off with his cousins and little black playmates on expeditions to Radnor Lake or Wild Man's Hill, will not, in fact, ever let him forget that he is "mostly a city boy, not on to country things like the others." And, though Quint in some ways seems to love the country, he comes to feel awkward and out-of-place there—eventually repudiating it altogether when, before the taunts of his city friends, he becomes ashamed of his grandfather's watch, which Grandma Lovell sends him for his twelfth birthday.

The first significant change in Quint's fortunes occurs when he is ten and his father is moved to St. Louis and begins a rapid rise in his company. In quick succession Gerald Dudley is made a vice president, is invited to join a country club and a men's town club, and meets the wealthy and charming Anna Lauterbach, the woman of means of the title. Mrs. Lauterbach, the only daughter of a St. Louis millionaire and the ex-wife of the heir to a brewery fortune, is perhaps more attracted to the prospective son she envisions in Quint than to the prospective husband she sees in Gerald. At any rate, Gerald Dudley soon weds her, and he and Quint then move into the monstrous Italian palace Mrs. Lauterbach's father had built for her the year she had made her debut.

Life at Casa Anna is all novelty for Quint. He has two pretty teenage stepsisters to amuse him. He has servants to wait on him. He attends a country day school during the year and spends summers at a Michigan resort. He is able to put down roots in a stable home environment. And, best of all, he finds a mother's love and solicitude lavished on him by his beautiful stepmother. Quint, with rare lyricism, recalls his feelings when he came into "practical possession of a mother":

> I thought of the peculiar happiness of loving her as I did, and I thought of the firmness with which I was established in her heart. Suddenly I had become the carefree hero of a wonderful adventure, and I was ready to have all the fun of it. It seemed that she had given me the power to breathe and that she was at the same time the breath

and the air breathed. And just as it is not necessary to remember to breathe in the midst of a foot race, from that day forward mere thoughts about her would become too tedious for me to bother with. (*WM*, 70–71)

So self-confident does Quint become in his new situation that he is able to establish himself as best-all-round boy in his division of the country day school and wins at the age of thirteen the coveted Dartmouth Cup on Class Day. But already the seeds of change have been planted. Personal conflicts begin to disrupt the idyllic menage. Gerald, who by this time has become president of his company, faces a showdown with the board of directors; disturbed by that problem, he is offended by a slight that he believes one of his adored stepdaughters shows him. He sulks off on a business trip and spoils a family holiday, not for the oblivious daughters, but for his wife and Quint. Gerald soon after proposes a South American vacation—as "amends," his wife believes—but cancels the plans when his board fires him. Because the news of the cancellation is broken to her while she is trying on her travel trousseau for him, Anna feels she has been deliberately humiliated by her husband, and a bitter quarrel ensues. Anna's suspicion that Gerald has married her for her money is renewed, even though Gerald refuses her invitation to him to manage her financial affairs and, in fact, takes a nonexecutive sales position with another company. So, too, is Gerald's suspicion renewed that Anna married him for his son.

Highly distraught and fearing that Gerald may try to take his son away, Anna begins to imagine herself pregnant and refuses to believe the doctors who deny that she is. Her neurotic withdrawal into fantasy is not suspected by Quint and Gerald, however, until she becomes physically ill one day and blames the illness on the imagined pregnancy. Her prognosis is not good, and her daughters finally decide to send her away to a sanitarium in the East and to dispose of her mansion by dismantling it and selling its components at auction. On the same day that news of Lindbergh's "amazing solo flight" across the Atlantic is announced, Quint sees his stepmother led away to the institution while the rest of the family debates the question of "Who's to blame?"

"The Amazing Solo Flight"

Without subplots and with its straightforward focus on a single family situation, the basic story of *A Woman of Means* is not very complicated. But the execution of the novel is, like Lindbergh's aeronautical feat, an "amazing solo flight" for a writer experienced only with short hauls. The narrative course, for one thing, is not plotted on a linear chart. The novel opens with a remembered scene of Quint's happy life in his stepmother's home: his stepsisters confiding secrets to their diaries, his father reveling in the girls' joshing chatter over a billiards table, his stepmother recalling incidents of her youth. But immediately we are shown Quint worrying about potential accidents that might spoil his blissful contentment, and the pathetic ending of the novel is already foreshadowed. For two and a half chapters of the four in the novel the narration moves back and forth from the more remote past of Quint's early childhood to the happy days with his new mother; from the middle of the third chapter to the end of the novel, the action moves more straightforwardly to its climax, with only an occasional anticipation of a future event or a passing allusion to a past one. The method is nothing radical or experimental (like, say, the "tunneling process" Virginia Woolf discovered in writing *Mrs. Dalloway*), but it is a particularly apt adaptation of what has almost become the conventional handling of time in the post-Jamesian novel.

What is perhaps most interesting in the structural technique is the surprising principle by which incidents in various periods of time are selected for dramatization. Many seemingly insignificant happenings are related in such detail that one expects latent significance: How will the girls' diaries figure in the plot? When will Miss Moore, the schoolteacher whom Quint's father dates briefly in St. Louis, pop up in Quint's life again? What will the Dartmouth Cup come to symbolize? But these are questions that lead nowhere; to ask them is, in fact, to misread the novel. Such questions assume that details of character and incident exist not for themselves, but for something more abstract, such as "story," "theme," or "preconceived effect," as indeed they might in much modern fiction. Taylor, however, allows his narrators a certain spontaneity in their introduction of detail, and this very openness and casualness enhances the verisimilitude of the narrative. People and events seem to be in a story not because they are intended to mean something but simply because they are a part of its reality.

And, as is usual in Peter Taylor's fiction, people are what we remember best about *A Woman of Means*. Several highly complex characterizations emerge in the short length of the novelette. The crucial one, of course, is Quint's, for it is through his consciousness that the other characters are seen and gain our interest. Quint, as a narrator, is no Holden Caulfield, no subjective adolescent still reacting to the experiences of an immediate past; he is, rather, more like Melville's Wellingboro Redburn, a mature adult detachedly reflecting on a process of maturation that took place some time ago. He neither bullies his audience into a reluctant intimacy nor holds it off with a cold formality. He is merely the necessary intermediary for experience that somehow seems worth re-creating.

Kenneth Clay Cathey has felt that Taylor has not "synthesized well enough" Quint's story with that of his stepmother. Cathey has complained also that too much of the earlier part of the novel is taken up with "exposition of the boy's life before his father's remarriage, exposition which really adds nothing to the understanding of his eventual psychological change." Cathey calls this a defect in novelistic form, a failure to depict especially in the stepmother, but also in Quint "a moral *evolution* instead of the moral *revelation* which is central to the short story."[3] But Quint does evolve, and the stages of his evolution are rather clearly marked by several key scenes. The first is when his father tries to tell him a "dream" he had one night of marrying again, and Quint realizes suddenly that he has always hated his father's "business drive" and realizes simultaneously that he himself is "the very center and core of it." The second is when his father announces his engagement, and Quint realizes that all the decisions that the rich widow and her daughters and his father may make in the future will inevitably affect him, that he is bound up in involuntary personal relationships. The third is when the headmaster identifies him as "Anna Lauterbach's boy" and leads Quint to the "practical possession of a mother" and a mother's love—to the voluntary acceptance of a binding relationship. The fourth scene in one sense reverses the direction of Quint's evolution, for it is when Quint wins the Dartmouth Cup and, annoyed and resentful of his stepmother's intrusion on the day of his personal triumph, asserts his independence by rejecting her silent demand to turn the cup over to her. And the final step in the evolution is Quint's beginning of his own Lindbergh-like solo flight on the day his stepmother is taken irrevocably away from him to the sanitarium. Quint has, in short, grown up through several important steps toward a mature independence.

The other characters, of course, are known to us only as Quint describes them, but their portraits are both vivid and credible. Grandma Lovell, for instance, has only a minor function in the plot, but she emerges in sharply etched lines in her few short scenes, especially in the one where she opposes Gerald's overprotectiveness of Quint. The physical images are sparse (we hear her talking "vaguely" of the values of country life, and we see her once retorting with her lips "suddenly drawn tight over her false teeth"), but the total impression of her inarticulate but implacable dignity is hardly dependent upon these. So, too, the teenage stepsisters, Bess and Laura, are brought to life with a great economy of technique: by tags of slangy speech ("Pardon me, I've got to go tell Diary something rich"), by incidental mention of their interests (collecting pillows and china dogs, planning holiday parties at the country club), by arrested images against a background ("They had wrapped themselves in their velvet capes, their voices had sounded crisp and thrilling in the hall for a moment, and then the heavy front door had slammed"). They are pretty, silly, and vain, and hence a stereotype; but they are also individuals whose actions, believable in retrospect, are not necessarily predictable in advance.

The most intriguing of the secondary characters is Quint's father, who sometimes seems transparently shallow, sometimes darkly complex. Gerald Dudley is in many ways the typical self-made American bourgeois, with the typical virtues ("an air of innocence," stoic dignity, diligence, perseverance, straightforward honesty) and the typical faults ("too austere integrity," stubborn pride, overzealous ambition, single-mindedness, preoccupation with success). Once, when Quint looks out a hotel window to see his father getting out of a taxi with two other businessmen, he thinks that he "could not have distinguished him from the other men on the sidewalk except for the old-fashioned broad-brimmed hat he wore." At another time Quint gets goose bumps noticing how exactly his father's expression is like those in the pictures of company officers and directors on the wall of his office.

Gerald Dudley is individuated, however, because he manifests personal attitudes that spring from hidden sources within him and because he enters into kinds of relationships that defy easy categorization. One conversation with Quint is especially revealing of the factors that formed him:

> He told me about the things he had learned when he was a farm boy himself and how it never helped him any to know those things when he went into business. "We had only a poor ridge farm," he said, "and we fought nature with nature. We always let the martins bin up in the eaves of our house to drive off the hawks. How they did use to scare me when they whizzed past my window upstairs at night. Our house was a real old timer with the eaves coming right down over the little square upstairs windows. There were no windows at all in the gables." He talked without sentiment, as though he were merely giving evidence. "There were always snakes in the corn crib to keep the rats away . . . . You learn a lot of things in the country, especially when there are no niggers around to get between you and the real work, but a mighty lot of good it did me when I went into hardware." (*WM,* 42)

Though the passage is at least partly ironical (learning to fight nature with nature has perhaps been part of Gerald's business success), it is also a credible subjective revelation. Gerald is capable of surprising us, too, by the delicate sensitivity of his affection for his stepdaughters, by his tender solicitude for his son, and by his resilient rise from his failure in business. The most convincing proof, moreover, that Taylor has not oversimplified this character lies in the fact that we can never answer with certainty the question that the stepmother raises: Did he really marry her only for her money? The evidence, even when carefully weighed and sifted, can tip the balance either way.

"A Spoiled Rich Woman"

Those who have found *A Woman of Means* disappointing have usually laid the blame on the characterization of the title character. Surely, Anna Lauterbach is the most beguiling and mysterious of all the personalities encountered in the book. She is in outward appearances beautiful, charming, talented, witty, gay, poised, contented—the farthest thing from the "corpulent little woman dressed in black" with pockmarked face, kinky bob, freckled arms, and stubby fingers loaded with diamonds whom Quint visualizes when first hearing of her. Inside, however, she is a bundle of frustrations and anxieties that finally produce the mental breakdown at the end of the novel. The artistic question is whether this denouement is sufficiently prepared for.

Careful attention to the details presented shows that Taylor has sprung no O. Henry-type surprises but has released forces that merely reach a natural, if not wholly foreseen, conclusion. Besides symbolic foreshadowing (Quint's morbid fear of a fatal accident in the family, for instance), Taylor gives ample clues that the stepmother's interior life is not so healthy as it might be. The first hint lies in the unusually strong attachment to her husband's son—an attachment strong enough to prompt Gerald's accusation that she married him just to get Quint. Whatever repressed sexual impulses may lie behind this attachment are only suggested, not exploited, by the author, and the relationship is open to interpretation on other levels. The second hint about Anna Lauterbach's inner state comes from the passages where she discusses her wealth and the paradoxical sense of insecurity that it has created in her. Her consciousness of her wealth came only when her schoolmates in Switzerland forced it: "I had never thought of our being rich before we left St. Louis and went to Europe," she tells Quint. But the schoolmates' constant behind-the-back references to her as "the American millionairess" built up a suspiciousness within her: "it seemed that that was all in me that interested them: my money" and "whenever I was about to invite some girl [as a companion on a holiday trip], she always said something that made me think she didn't like me for myself."

Anna Lauterbach's desire for a son, then, is at least partially a desire for someone who will love her for herself, the way her own father loved her when he built Casa Anna for her. She does not find this kind of love in her first marriage to the brewery heir (whom she treats like a little boy) or even in her second marriage to Gerald Dudley. She thinks she has found it in Quint until his burgeoning desire for adult independence asserts itself. And this disappointment brings her final mental collapse: having failed to attain her desires in reality, she turns to fantasy and imagines herself to be carrying in her womb the son who will love her for herself. At the climax of the novel, then, she repeats the old accusation once more, this time to Quint. "You deceitful little wretch," she cries to him, "you're plotting with the rest of them to smother my baby! And *you*'re after my money, too!" It is not so much the hysterical pregnancy as this final rejection of reality that marks her complete psychological disintegration.

All of the characterizations in *A Woman of Means* have several features in common. In the first place, none of them is simply a stereotype, though each bears some obvious traits of a character type. Yet Anna Lauterbach cannot be explained with the easy label "spoiled rich woman" that Gerald pins on her in a quarrel, any more than Gerald can be adequately explained as an American bourgeois or Bess and Laura as fickle teenagers. Furthermore, the characters do not fall into neat moral categories: there are no heroes or villains in this novel. Not a single character is completely unsympathetic and not a single character is without moral flaws. Nor are the characters mere emblems of other things, without interest in themselves but important only in their symbolic frame. They exist as people truthfully re-created from the real world, and they become known and defined precisely by their complicated interactions with other characters and with their environment.

On Its Own Terms

Because the Taylor style in *A Woman of Means* (as, indeed, in most of his other works) suggests an oral conversation, it presents the subject with an anecdotal objectivity that seldom makes explicit its thematic significance. "This is how it was," Taylor seems to say through his narrator, not "This is what it means." As a result, readers of *A Woman of Means*, however satisfying they may have found the novelette as a re-creation of experience, may find it difficult to pinpoint its insights into life or even to identify its literary type.

There are several types of book *A Woman of Means* might have, but did not, become. It is most emphatically not a naturalistic account of bourgeois manners and morals. Although it is firmly grounded in realistic detail, verifiable by any observer of American life, the novel lacks the detachment to process its narrative material as quasi-scientific data; Anna Lauterbach may in some externals resemble the heroines of John O'Hara, but she is a fictional creation of an entirely different order. Neither is the novel clinical, however much the Phaedra theme might have invited the amateur psychoanalysis so prevalent in modern fiction. Certainly, Anna's obsessive, perhaps erotic, predilection for her stepson, her immature relationships to her father and her two husbands, her hysterical pregnancy, her developing paranoia, and her eventual disorientation from reality could be greatly elucidated by Freudian theories. Still, Taylor's interest in Anna is not psychiatric; he nowhere gives the impression of attempting a clinical study of a neurotic's psychological disintegration.

The sociological is of even less concern than the psychological. Despite a clear-cut class contrast among his principal characters, Taylor does not exploit the potential for social satire. Gerald never quite becomes a Babbitt-like caricature, Laura and Bess parodies of comic strip teenagers, or Anna a burlesque of the American millionairess. Even the snobbery Quint encounters at the country day school is presented dispassionately as objective reality with little or no comment or evaluation, explicit or implicit. Similarly, this novel (unlike many other novels by contemporary Southerners) avoids historical allegory. Though Anna wins Quint away from Grandma Lovell, Taylor does not let his novel become a mere parable recounting the old-fashioned South's loss of its sons to the progressive Midwest, the replacement of the agrarian ideal by the urban-industrial fact, or the wooing and unfortunate wedding of outside capital by New South opportunism. While the novel is in some degree susceptible to each of these semiallegorical interpretations, such meanings provide only overtones, not major harmonics.

Finally, this story of a youth's awakening avoids also the pitfalls of the sentimental bildungsroman, which are such a peril to so many first novelists. It is only retrospectively, in fact, that the reader becomes aware that this is primarily Quint's story and that the pattern has followed closely the pattern of many another novel of adolescent experiences. Perhaps because Quint is younger and less self-conscious than most bildungsroman heroes, perhaps because he shares the stage with the more dramatic character of his stepmother, perhaps because Taylor's delicate irony is ever spare and wary of excess, *A Woman of Means* escapes the romantic subjectivity that has been the ruin of so many of its prototypes.

If Peter Taylor has written neither a naturalistic document nor a clinical study nor a sociological diatribe nor a historical allegory nor a sentimental bildungsroman, what has he written? The answer is simple, but evasive: he has written a novel that, like all good works of art, can be fully comprehended only on its own individual terms, not in the generic terms of a literary type. Hence, the apparent thematic ambiguity of it—we find ourselves as reluctant to try to explain this vicarious experience as we would to explain a real-life complex of events. The joy is in the aesthetic contemplation, not in the philosophical exposition.

Chapter Four
The Widows of Thornton

"A Simple Country Town"

The eight stories and one short play included in *The Widows of Thornton* (1954)[1] were all published originally in magazines between November 1948 and March 1954. Since an apprenticeship of at least a dozen years lies behind even the earliest of these pieces, it is not surprising to find Peter Taylor emerging as a master craftsman. *The Widows of Thornton,* however, is more than just the next expected step in a promising writer's career. Though *A Long Fourth* and *A Woman of Means* both revealed unquestioned talent, neither quite fully indicated the precise form in which this talent would find its most congenial expression. Certain longish stories like "The Scoutmaster" and "A Long Fourth," for instance, suggested that the novel might be the natural genre for the channeling of Taylor's gifts, but the novelette *A Woman of Means,* appealing as it was in many of its parts, did not have essentially novelistic virtues. Stories like "Allegiance" and "Sky Line" held the promise that Taylor might break ground with experimental techniques; stories like "The Fancy Woman" and "A Spinster's Tale" hinted that he might explore unusual or aberrant sociological and psychological situations. In short, Peter Taylor's second story collection could have taken any of several directions.

What is so amazing about *The Widows of Thornton* is the artistic homogeneity of the pieces in it: it is as if the writer had never for one moment considered any other form for it, as if his chosen style and themes had been born fully formed, Venus-like, from the muddy foam of the Tennessee River. Gone are the arty mannerisms, slightly melodramatic contrivances, vaguely Gothic settings, and overtly dramatic confrontations and reversals that cropped up occasionally in the earlier work. Chronology is still much manipulated (as it was, for example, in "The Scoutmaster"), but there is no sense of fanciful distortion or neo-Proustian experimentation. Characters are economically developed but fully individuated; background detail is abundant and credibly authentic; plots seem to spring naturally from character and setting. Although Taylor had already shown himself a master of the first-person point of view (and would come to use that point of view more and more in his later work), he eschews it completely in this volume and relies principally on the third-person, central intelligence viewpoint, which he develops with the same kind of comfortable leisureliness—colloquial and apparently digressive—that had already distinguished "The Scoutmaster" and "A Long Fourth." Overall, Taylor's technical prowess in *The Widows of Thornton* has become so controlled it gives the illusion of complete artlessness.

The thematic concerns, moreover, are narrowed down from the comparatively wide-ranging interests of *A Long Fourth,* but consequently are probed more deeply. The original conception of the book was more sociological than the final product, according to Taylor's own account:

> My idea was to write a group of stories dealing with the histories of four or five families from a country town [Thornton, Tennessee] who had migrated, during a period of twenty-five years, to various cities of the South and Midwest . . . . I wanted to present these families—both Negro and white—living a modern urban life while continuing to be aware of their old identities and relationships. I wanted to give the reader the impression that every character carried in his head a map of that simple country town while going about his life in the complex city. I wanted to show, in fact, how old patterns, for good or bad, continued to dominate many aspects of these people's lives. In writing the individual stories I discovered new themes in them and found that I sometimes wanted to write directly about the old town itself.[2]

Taylor stuck to his original plan in that he set two of the pieces in St. Louis, two in Nashville, one each in Detroit and Chicago, and one on a train outside Memphis. Though all the stories have characters who apparently derive from Thornton, only two—"What You Hear from 'Em?" and "Cookie"—have the principal action set in the town of Thornton itself.

The sociocultural themes that do emerge are hardly Faulknerian: there is little of the epic-style mythologizing so often associated with the "Southern school" of modern fiction. It is made clear, though, that Thornton—"the old, dying town on the bluffs above the Tennessee River"—is a pervasive presence in the lives of all the characters, just as its prototype—Trenton, Tennessee, Taylor's birthplace—has been in Taylor's life. As the protagonist of "The Dark Walk" discovers, life in the strange, vague cities where rural Southerners so often find themselves today exists only as the opposite of something else—the remembered life of a particular place of origin, like Thornton:

> It was there that she had known the name and quality of everything. It was there, more than anywhere else, that everything had a name. Not only the streets and alleys there had names; there had been names for the intersections of streets: Wifeworking Corner, the Blocks, the Stepdown. Not only the great houses and small houses had

names; on the outskirts of the town were two abandoned barns known as the Hunchback's Barn and General Forrest's Stable. (*WT,* 301–2)

Thornton provides for these stories what Eudora Welty has defined as "place": "the named, identified, concrete, exact and exacting, and therefore credible, gathering spot of all that has been felt, is about to be experienced" in the progress of a fiction. When the reader can accept the "place" of a fiction as "true," Welty says, then "through it will begin to glow, in a kind of recognizable glory, the feeling and thought that inhabited . . . the author's head and animated the whole of his work."[3]

Taylor's town of Thornton functions more like Welty's Morgana, Mississippi, in *The Golden Apples,* than like Faulkner's Yoknapatawpha County: it grounds the stories in concrete actuality, but does not create any special mythic transcendence of time and place. Taylor focuses on Thornton not as a sociopolitical community, but as the source of familial and class values and traditions. Once again he is obsessed with domestic relationships: the interplay of parents, children, servants, dependent kinfolk. The household of a fictional Taylor family like the Tollivers or the Wades is never the statistically average nuclear family; the numbers are swollen by extra children, uncles, aunts, assorted other female relatives or companions, maids, chauffeurs, cooks, houseboys. Individual characters may have their own special personality traits, but to a large degree their identities derive from the roles they have been assigned and the moral heritage they have been bequeathed from their family's origins in the country town.

"All That Was Old and Useless and Inherited"

The story that most explicitly presents the unifying theme of *The Widows of Thornton* is "The Dark Walk," the last (and the longest) story of the volume.[4] It reveals that the title of the collection is not a literal description of the heroines, but a startling metaphor.

"The Dark Walk" is the story of Sylvia Harrison, the only actual widow in the book. Sylvia is introduced at an apparently inconsequential but quite revealing point in her life where many of her traits are brought into relief. The time is the mid-1930s when Sylvia is already the mother of four children, the oldest of whom is sixteen. The reader discovers her at an insufferably old-fashioned Colorado resort—the kind of place where entertainment consists of a depressing Saturday night dance where "twelve-year-old girls, still wearing sashes and patent-leather pumps, danced with their grandfathers" and "worse still, old ladies danced together and 'broke' on each other."

The reason that Sylvia has chosen this resort instead of Colorado Springs (which the "sensible" parents of her children's school friends chose) is a key to Sylvia's character. This resort, it seems, is run by old Miss Katty Moore, who is a native of Sylvia's home state of Tennessee and who had taught gymnastics at Ward-Belmont School in Nashville when Sylvia was a student there. Grotesquely formidable as she now is (shingled snow-white hair, white satin evening dress with low-quarter white tennis shoes, eyes coyly rolling back into her head until only the whites show), the incredibly muscular old lady is to Sylvia an "association" with the past, something to write to her old schoolmates about, something of Tennessee carried over into the present life. As Sylvia is gradually revealed to the reader, it becomes obvious that the loyalty to old Miss Katty is just one manifestation of a deeply ingrained character trait.

Sylvia has developed her attitude toward Tennessee over the course of many moves throughout the South and Midwest as the career of her husband, Nate, took him to bigger and bigger jobs and to larger and larger cities. Always in these moves, ever since the first one from Cedar Springs to Memphis, Sylvia has carted some four vans of furniture—"almost everything in the way of furniture that her family or Nate's had ever owned." She has developed what is almost a mystique about moving, baffling friends and family by her "untroubled and independent spirit at movingtime," organizing the logistics of the move all by herself, priding herself on her efficient technique. Though some things remain ever crated in attic or warehouse, the furniture she transfers from house to house always dominates any new interior so that individuality is completely obscured and her family can hardly realize its surroundings have been changed. "Home was not Chicago or Detroit, or any of the other places they had lived," Sylvia thus implies. "Home was the old Harrison place at Cedar Springs, or perhaps Sylvia's own family house at Thornton." Furthermore, there is always the understanding that someday the Harrisons will all go back to Tennessee.

Life in the Tennessee small towns from which Sylvia and her husband came is not, however, very appealing in the real-life examples Sylvia sees in the homes of her old acquaintances. She inevitably pities each old schoolmate, finding that the typical husband seems to have "retired from the social scene in Thornton," insisting on his right to be like other modern men while demanding at the same time that "his wife, Sylvia's girlhood friend, must continue to live as she always has." Strangely, Sylvia recalls Nate's saying when they were first engaged that "everything changes so fast in our country that a smart person can't hold on to the past—not to any part of it if he wants to be a success." Still, she cherishes the "bittersweet tone" of the "pleasant, prosperous, pastoral surroundings" of Middle Tennessee circa 1915, where "she had seen everything that was good in the noble past of her country meeting head on with everything that was exciting and marvelous about the twentieth century."

Sylvia's reassessment of her attitudes is necessitated by the sudden death of her husband in Chicago in 1939 when she is forty-four. Everyone assumes, of course, that Sylvia will now make the long-intended return to Tennessee, and she herself begins dutiful preparations. About this point, though, Sylvia begins to entertain separately two masculine callers: the first is her elderly landlord, Mr. Canada, an undeclared suitor who tries to persuade her to stay in Chicago; the other is Leander, the black chauffeur, who was one of the servants accompanying Sylvia from Cedar Springs in her first move twenty years earlier and who is now asking her to let him go back to Tennessee with her. Sylvia's children tease her about her "Black Knight" and her "White Knight," but Sylvia sees the two men as representing for her "the two sides of a rather simple question, the question of whether or not it was wise of her to be taking her family back to Tennessee."

At first concerned about her own selfishness, Sylvia eventually realizes that neither side of the question is really her own:

> *She* had no side, no voice in the argument, and had never had one. The two voices she had been listening to for weeks past had both been Nate's voice. They were voices she had heard for years and years. The two men, quarreling in her back hall, seemed to represent the two sides of Nate. He had, through all the years, *wanted* her to *want* to go back to Tennessee. That was what his tolerance had meant. Her own wishes had never entered into it. That was what Nate's tolerance had meant. It had meant his freedom from a part of himself, a part of himself that would have bound him to a place and to a past time otherwise inescapable. He had *wanted* her to insist upon taking all that furniture everywhere they went. . . . She felt now an immense weariness, felt as though she had been carrying all that absurd furniture on her back these twenty years. And for what purpose? Why, so that Nate might be free to live that part of life in which there somehow must be no furniture. His selfishness, for the moment, seemed so monstrous to her that she almost smiled at the judgments she had passed upon herself. (*WT,* 298)

With this new awareness, Sylvia reaches her decision: she sends the vans of furniture and Leander back to Tennessee without her, and she takes a brand-new apartment in Chicago to be filled with "new and useful and pleasing" furnishings that she herself will select. She will retain nothing to remind her "of the necessity there had been to dispense with all that was old and useless and inherited."

"All, Somehow, Widows"

"The Dark Walk" would have been interesting enough if this were the extent of its revelations. But embodied in the telling of the story are two significant images that lead to further meanings. The first is the image that provides the title for the story; the second is the image that provides the title for the whole volume. The Dark Walk is the overgrown riverside path in Thornton where courting couples used to stroll, the very spot where Nate had proposed. Besides its association with romantic bliss, the Dark Walk has a more sinister connotation: "an element of mystery and danger . . . in the bright colored spiders which sometimes spun their webs across the path or in the fat water moccasins hurrying innocently across the path into the rank growth of creeper and poison ivy." It is the recalling of these paradoxical associations with the Dark Walk that leads Sylvia to the second key image: the bride-widow paradox.

Ever since her youth Sylvia has cherished "the image of herself as a young girl in white dimity repeating and sharing the experience of all the other girls to whom life had seemed to begin anew" in the Dark Walk. At the point of her life where she realizes the role she has been forced to play by her husband's silent demands, Sylvia finds the image has changed:

> She and the other young girls no longer seemed to be beginning life anew in the Dark Walk. They were all dressed in black, and it seemed that the experience they had shared there was really the beginning of widowhood. From the moment they pledged their love they were all, somehow, widows; and she herself had become a widow not the day Nate was found dead in his office but the day he asked her to marry him, in the Dark Walk. It seemed to her that in some way or other all the men of that generation in that town had been killed in the old war of her grandfather's day. Or they had been set free by it. Or their lives had been changed in a way that the women's lives were not changed. The men of Nate's time had crossed over a border, had pushed into a new country, or fled into a new country. And their brides lived as widows clinging to things the men would never come back to and from which they could not free themselves. Nate had gone literally to a new country, but Sylvia knew in her heart that it would have been the same if they had never left Cedar Springs. (*WT,* 303–4)

Pledging love, then, for a woman in Sylvia's sociocultural context, means a clinging to the "old and useless and inherited"—the four vans of furniture Sylvia moved from city to city. The men escape to freedom (even the husbands of Sylvia's schoolmates back in Thornton, we remember, have retired from the scene, seeming almost not to be there at all), but Sylvia and the other wives must live as they always have. The "widows" of Thornton are the futile bearers of vain tradition in a changing modern world.

The majority of the stories in *The Widows of Thornton* can be seen as more or less related extensions of this central theme. Two stories directly concern wives who are in Sylvia's sense "somehow widows," and three others deal with various women who, in pledging their love, were led to cling to something from which they might otherwise have been free.

One of the simplest stories, "Cookie" (originally entitled "Middle Age"), takes on a significance in the context of the whole volume that it probably would not have alone. It presents a wife who is a very paragon of patience and servility trying to preserve the slender ties that bind her philandering doctor-husband to her. "Two nights a week, he *had* to be home for supper, and some weeks, when his conscience was especially uneasy, he turned up three or four times," the story begins; and we meet the husband and wife at a typical evening meal. The dull chronic tensions between the two are subtly revealed underneath ritualistic conversational banalities:

> He served himself from the dish of beans and selected a piece of the side meat. He bent his head over and got one whiff of the steaming dish. "You're too good to me," he said evenly. He pushed the dish across the table to within her reach.
>
> "Nothing's too good for one's husband."
>
> "You're much too good to me," he said, now lowering his eyes to his plate. (*WT,* 152; *ML,* 390; *CS,* 282)

The dramatic catalyst in the story is the title character, the black cook, who is completely dedicated to her mistress. Goaded by the petty teasing of her mistress's husband, Cookie cunningly lets slip, in feigned innocence, an allusion to the husband's infidelities, bringing into the open what had before been hidden. Both husband and wife, however, choose to take the indiscretion as an example of "old-nigger uppitiness" and to ignore its implications for their situation. As the wife goes out to remonstrate with Cookie, the doctor-husband flees the house once more, reflecting on their "ugly, old voices," their "senseless voices"—"the righteousness and disillusion of Cookie's, the pride and discipline of his wife's." Like Nate in "The Dark Walk," he leaves his wife behind, a virtual prisoner in her conventional home; and he turns himself toward the symbol of his own escape: "In the driveway, his car, bright and new and luxurious, was waiting for him."

Just as the wives in "The Dark Walk" and "Cookie" are figurative widows without knowing it, so too is the heroine of "A Wife of Nashville." The title appropriately focuses our attention on what is of most evident significance about her: first, her social role as wife; second, her cultural context of Southern city life. Her name, Helen Ruth, suggests that she contains at least potentially the contrasting attributes of both of the great prototypes of wifehood: the faithless pagan Helen and the faithful biblical Ruth. Helen Ruth is, in fact, a study of the debilitating kind of vague female dissatisfaction that Betty Friedan would popularize, fifteen years after this story was written, in *The Feminine Mystique.*

Developed as a seemingly anecdotal chronicle of a housewife's dealings with various household servants over a period of more than twenty years, "A Wife of Nashville" only gradually reveals its underlying pattern. As Helen Ruth frets in turn over lazy Jane Blakemoor, shifty and negligent Carrie, religious but amorous Sarah, and devoted but deceptive Jess McGeehee, she is really fretting over her own lot as wife. "It seemed to her then that she had so little in life that she was entitled to the satisfaction of keeping an orderly house and to the luxury of efficient help," we are told. "There was too much else she had not had—an 'else' nameless to her, yet sorely missed—for her to be denied these small satisfactions." The black servants always eventually leave her house; their length of service ranges from nearly three years to a full eight years. Even Jess McGeehee, who "idealized the family" and kept a scrapbook on the accomplishments of Helen Ruth's three boys, finally sets up an elaborate subterfuge and departs for California. But, except for a brief and only vaguely defined separation once in the early years of her marriage, Helen Ruth has remained tied to her household, despite her wistful yearning for a nameless "so much else."

The irony is that the whole world, including presumably Helen Ruth's own husband and children, believes her marriage ideal. "It's too bad more marriages can't be like theirs, each living their own life," a friend observes. "Everyone admires it as a real achievement." But what irks Helen Ruth is that in fact only John R., her husband, leads an independent life. Away most of the week on business trips, John R. runs away at other times on hunting and fishing trips, takes her only to parties with his hunting friends, and, when at home, piles up on the bed after supper and sleeps. (Only for a brief period during the Great Depression when John R. "had to give up all his 'activities' and devote his entire time to selling insurance," did Helen Ruth find herself "spending all her evenings playing Russian bank with a man who had no interest in anything but his home, his wife, and his three boys." But during this period, John R. develops psychosomatic back pains.)

Helen Ruth at first believed that she was "perfectly happy with her present life" but that John R. must be "unhappy" since he seemed no longer to enjoy her company. Hence there was more than once some talk of separation and divorce during the first two years of their marriage and even one actual brief separation when Helen Ruth returned to Thornton with her two babies and Carrie. "Their reconciliation," we are told, "whatever it meant to John R., meant to her the acceptance of certain mysteries—the mystery of his love of hunting, of his choice of friends, of his desire to maintain a family and home of which he saw so little, of his attachment to her, and of her own devotion to him."

If Helen Ruth had been vouchsafed the insight granted to Sylvia Harrison in "The Dark Walk," she might have penetrated the sociological center of these "mysteries." As it is, she submits to the specious reasoning of her women friends: "Because a woman's husband hunts is no reason for her to hunt, any more than because a man's wife sews is any reason for him to sew." Only when the final servant, Jess McGeehee, the one they had thought would one day be called "Mammy" by future grandchildren, leaves them does Helen Ruth plumb something of her life's "mysteries"—but her insight is psychological rather than sociological.

As the only member of the family to discern Jess's reasons for leaving, Helen Ruth tries to explain the unexpected departure to her husband and son. Why should Jess, who had "no life of her own," pack up and leave forever her beloved white family? The answer is, of course, that it is too unnatural for anyone, even a Jess McGeehee or a Helen Ruth Lovell, to have *no* life of her own. But the answer is also to be found in the essential "loneliness" that people feel. Helen Ruth would gladly draw illustrations from her own life if she could only make her family understand:

> If it would make them see what she had been so long in learning to see, she would even talk at last about the "so much else" that had been missing from her life and that she had not been able to name, and about the foolish mysteries she had so nobly accepted upon her reconciliation with John R. To her, these things were all one now; they were her loneliness, the loneliness from which everybody, knowingly or unknowingly, suffered. But she knew that her husband and her sons did not recognize her loneliness or Jess McGeehee's or their own. (*WT,* 98; *ML,* 307–8; *CS,* 279–80)

Despairing of communicating her insight to her family, Helen Ruth finally turns away from the "identical expressions, not of wonder but of incredulity" on the masculine faces; and she pushes her teacart into the dining room, the symbolic center of her life and that of Jess McGeehee. The dining room is "spotlessly clean, the way Jess McGeehee had left it," but it is also—as the visible representation of the frigid widowish underworld to which a wife of

Nashville is doomed—a kind of dark walk, "dark and cool as an underground cavern."

It is a part of Peter Taylor's artistry that a story such as this is not reducible to just another post-Ibsenite plea to release latter-day Noras from their doll houses. There are no polemics in "A Wife of Nashville" or in the other stories of *The Widows of Thornton;* there are almost no judgments or commentaries on the situations so skillfully elucidated. Sylvia Harrison in "The Dark Walk" is the only heroine to make a rebellious decision, and even this decision comes when the circumstances have already substantially changed. The wives in "Cookie" and "A Wife of Nashville" merely endure their situations, which, perhaps, they have come to understand a little better. If Southern family customs make all wives widows in their husband's houses, Taylor is not quixotic enough to offer a panacea for the problem.

"They Ought to Come Home"

Perhaps Taylor's reticence is in deference to the complexity and extensiveness of the problem. As several other pieces in *The Widows of Thornton* show, the metaphoric widowhood may fall on others besides wives. Old family servants, dependent maiden aunts, rich benefactresses, and devoted daughters and nieces can also—by "pledging their love" to a family—enter the dark walk to spiritual widowhood, clinging to things the rest of the world values no more.

The much-anthologized "What You Hear from 'Em?" is one of the most poignant of such stories—the account of Aunt Munsie, the aged black mammy of one of the "quality" families in Thornton, the Tollivers. "Without being able to book-read or even to make numbers, she had finished raising the whole pack of towheaded Tollivers just as the Mizziz would have wanted it done," we are told. "The Doctor told her she *had* to—he didn't ever think about getting another wife, or taking in some cousin, not after his 'Molly darling'—and Aunt Munsie *did.*" In the "halcyon days after the old Mizziz had died," Aunt Munsie's word had actually "become law in the Tolliver household."

The story deals, however, with the period of the 1920s after Aunt Munsie's white charges have grown up, moved away, and begun families of their own. It is the moving away that has most grieved Munsie and that prompts the reiterated question she poses to the few remaining white people who understand it: "What you hear from 'em?" By this query, she wants to know only when her two favorites of the Tolliver children, Mr. Thad and Mr. Will, are going to "pack up their families and come back to Thornton for good." The letters, the Christmas presents, and the occasional ritual visits she gets from Mr. Thad and Mr. Will and their families mean nothing to her; she is looking for their permanent return and nothing less satisfies her.

Munsie realizes that the Tolliver boys—like many other Thornton scions "who had gone off somewhere making money"—are "prospering" in their fine businesses in Memphis and Nashville. But she feels that, "if they were going to be rich, they ought to come home, where their granddaddy had owned land and where their money counted for something." Otherwise, they are only like the mill manager from Chicago, who has "a yard full of big cars and a stucco house as big as you like" but whom nobody in Thornton would take for "rich." Though the old Tolliver house, left vacant by the heirs, has long ago burned down, Munsie insists there is still a sharp division between real "quality" families like her Tollivers and "has-been quality," "mill-hands," and "strangers from up North who [run] the Piggly Wiggly, the five-and-ten-cent store, and the roller-skating rink."

It is a "conspiracy" that takes place in the town—a conspiracy directed toward Aunt Munsie's own good—that finally forces the old woman to face the truth. The conspiracy, launched by some of the quality ladies of the town and abetted by Mr. Will and Mr. Thad's intercession with the mayor, is a plot to get a law passed banning pigs in the city limits, so that Munsie will have no reason to push her traffic-disrupting slop wagon through the streets. Whether or not her own safety was the motivation for the action, Munsie finds the Tolliver part in the conspiracy a revelation. "I tell you what the commotion's about," she says the day she drives away her pigs. "They *ain't* comin' back. They ain't never comin' back. They ain't never had no notion of comin' back." She rejects at the same time any idea that she might go to them, because, as she puts it to her collie dog, "I ain't nothin' to 'em in Memphis, and they ain't nothin' to me in Nashville." "*You* can go!" she irately informs the dog. "A collie dog's a collie dog anywhar. But Aunt Munsie, she's just their Aunt Munsie here in Thornton. I got mind enough to see *that*."

Thus, old and ignorant as she is, Aunt Munsie reaches a profound truth about the relative value of social roles. Up to this point she has lived the role her station in the Tolliver household permitted; she had a hard pride and dignity that at least the quality folks of the town could understand. But in the twenty years she lives on after the end of her daily rounds with the slop wagon, in the twenty years before she dies at the reputed age of one hundred, she lives a changed role. People say she has "softened," for she laughs and hollers with the white folks on the Square "the way they liked her to," takes to tying a bandanna about her head, begins talking "old-nigger foolishness," reminisces about the Civil War and about the old days in the Tolliver family, maintains a new formality toward Mr. Thad and Mr. Will and their families, and never again asks any more about when they are "sure enough coming back." Recognizing that the context for her role has disappeared, she has, in short, adapted at the age of eighty-two to the circumstances of a changing world.

"What You Hear from 'Em?" brings to life the whole complex of racial and social stratifications in the small-town South, while avoiding the opposite dangers of sentimental idealization and nervous condescension. It is also a paean to human dignity, a lament for the passing of the small town, and a variant comment on the "widowhood" theme of the previously discussed stories. This time we realize that the movement of the sons of the South into a "new country" leaves more than their wives clinging to the "old and useless and inherited," and that not the least of those useless things are social roles adapted to a context that will never be revived.

"How This Family Business Works"

Successful accommodations to changed contexts can sometimes be made—at least for a while, as the one short play in *The Widows of Thornton* demonstrates. *The Death of a Kinsman* is the dramatization of a crucial moment in the life of an expatriate Tennessee family in Detroit, a moment when carefully preserved "roles" are brought up for reexamination. The large Wade household—consisting of Robert, his wife Margie, his Aunt Lida, his five children, and three black servants—has managed to preserve in alien surroundings a Southern way of life based on models of an earlier day. The most delicate roles, those which have to be enacted with the greatest tact and consciousness of the unwritten rules, are of course the ones of the wife and the dependent female relative: the traditionally problematic two women under one roof.

Fortunately, Margie and Aunt Lida play their roles without a cross word to mar the family serenity. "It's because we have arranged our lives as we have," Margie explains to her husband. "It's because Aunt Lida and I have played our roles so perfectly, as we've always seen them played in Tennessee: She, the maiden aunt, responsible and capable! I, the beautiful young wife, the bearer of children, the reigning queen!" Conceivably, the arrangement might have lasted indefinitely, had an external force not brought a challenge to it.

This force is the opinion of the modern, urban, non-Southern culture, represented in the person of Miss Bluemeyer, the Yankee housekeeper. "When I selected Miss Bluemeyer for Margie's housekeeper," Aunt Lida says, "I was careful to choose someone who wouldn't fit in. If she were congenial with us, her presence here would be an intrusion. That's why my presence is an intrusion, don't you see?" Being totally outside the Southern tradition, Miss Bluemeyer has difficulty recognizing the clearly defined "spheres of authority" in the house and seems to the Wades "critical and questioning of a happy family life."

The death of an estranged and misanthropic relative, a Cousin Harry Wilson, is the event that brings Miss Bluemeyer and Aunt Lida into open conflict. With typical Southern concern for the obligations of "kinship," the Wades begin the obsequies for Cousin Harry, much to the mystification of Miss Bluemeyer. The housekeeper at first thinks the Wades are "such wonderful people to feel so responsible for a person they hardly know," but she later concludes that they are only fawning over a relative in an impersonal and meaningless Southern ritual. Believing that she is the only one who has any concern for the dead man as a person, Miss Bluemeyer sends flowers anonymously to the funeral service, a gesture that brings only a snide rebuff from Aunt Lida.

"What is it about Miss Bluemeyer's queerness that disturbs Aunt Lida so?" Robert Wade innocently asks, and Margie replies: "It is simply that someone has entered the field who won't play the game according to Aunt Lida's rules." Aunt Lida puts it another way; it is people like the embittered Cousin Harry and Miss Bluemeyer, she says, who make the role-playing "hard," who "point an accusing finger." Inevitably, the confrontation of the two women must occur, and when it does Miss Bluemeyer dramatically gives her notice:

MISS BLUEMEYER: . . . I understand a good deal of how this family business works. It makes a woman safe and sure being related this way and that way to everybody around her. And it keeps you from having to bother about anybody else, since they are not "kinfolks." I understand how it works, for I was one of nine, and I saw the women in my family making the most of it too. And I might have done the same, but I was a queer sort who couldn't make herself do it.

AUNT LIDA: Is that all, Miss Bluemeyer?

MISS BLUEMEYER: Not quite all. For a solid year I have watched you here giving directions and making this house your own. And I have seen it right along that you are really the same as I in lots of your feelings, Miss Wade, that you are really lost and alone in the world, but you would not have it

> so, you just wouldn't. All along I have seen you are really a brainy woman and yet to see you here saying the things you say and play-acting all the time! And then when the old man Wilson was dying, you, like the rest of 'em, talked of nothing but that he was kin, kin, kin. You have mocked and joked all this day and gave him a funeral only because he was a kinsman. (*WT,* 147–48; *ML,* 243; *OF,* 355–56)

The point of the play, then, is that Aunt Lida and Miss Bluemeyer are indeed "really the same" in many ways—only the accommodation each has made to circumstances has been different. Aunt Lida has chosen the way of the Southern gentlewoman, assuming the role of dependent relative with its small prerogatives and large heartaches. But this role is possible only by clinging to the remnants of a lost past—the familiar plight of Taylor's other "widows." Miss Bluemeyer, on the other hand, has chosen the way Southern men of the past few generations (but not Southern women) have been choosing: the way of independent enterprise in a mobile society. To the Southern-bred woman, Miss Bluemeyer's way seems a reveling in "bitterness" and a despising of all those who try to make life "a less lonesome, a less dreary business," while to the Northern-bred woman, Aunt Lida's way seems an abject surrender of all "pride and independence."

"Life's Most Important Lessons"

One story, "Two Ladies in Retirement," presents both alternatives successively in the same woman. The woman is Miss Betty Pettigru, a Nashville society leader for twenty-five years, who suddenly retires with a female cousin and close companion to the home of some relatives in St. Louis. One of the most memorable characters Taylor has created (she appears again in the play *Tennessee Day in St. Louis*), Miss Betty is a combination of Aunt Lida's craving for familial affection and Miss Bluemeyer's yen for independence. Unfortunately, she has the Southern woman's usual difficulty in realizing both desires.

In Nashville Miss Betty had made the most of her none-too-promising opportunities. As "the unbeautiful, untalented heiress of a country family's fortune" removed from the "decaying and disappearing" country town (Thornton) that gave that fortune its only meaning, she had little chance of fulfilling her father's injunction to make her "place" in "the heart of some gentle, honest man." Instead, she did what a man might have done:

> The men of her generation, and of later generations, had gone to Nashville, Memphis, Louisville, and even to St. Louis, and had used their heads, their connections, and their genteel manners to make their way to the top in the new order of things. And wasn't that all *she* had done, and in the only way permissible for a Miss Pettigru from Thornton? Once the goal was defined, was it necessary that she should be any less ruthless than her male counterparts? In her generation, the ends justified the means. For men, at least, they did. Now, at last, Miss Betty saw how much like a man's life her own had been. (*WT,* 186–87; *OF,* 312–13)

What Miss Betty had done was to build her life on a hardheaded personal goal—social climbing—through a ruthless process of what her companion Flo Dear thought of as "sin and expiation, sin and expiation, but with never a resolution to sin no more" and what Miss Betty herself thought of as "life, plain and simple, where you did what good things you could and what bad things you must."

Finally, facing at last the fact of the "worthlessness" of the goal that circumstances and personal limitations had set for her, Miss Betty abandoned Nashville society to take up permanent residence with the James Tolliver family in St. Louis where she could hope to indulge time, money, and love on three young nephews. Here, however, as the story opens, Miss Betty finds she has strong competition for the favor of the three Tolliver boys. Her rival, ironically enough, is Vennie, the Tollivers' aging cook, who lures the children with special treats cooked on her "magic stove" in her basement apartment and captivates them with exciting stories about old times in Thornton.

There is little doubt that Miss Betty will eventually triumph over old Vennie; the question is "To what means will she stoop to do it?" The temptation to win a quick victory by slightly less than honorable methods is not long in coming, and it comes from a particularly charming tempter, one of the very prizes over whom the contest is being waged. Vance, the oldest boy, has been offended, it seems, by some of Vennie's joshing in front of his school friends. Sensing his aunt's own attitude toward Vennie, he gives Miss Betty the opportunity to eavesdrop through a hot-air register on "carryings-on" in Vennie's apartment and insinuates that incriminating evidence sufficient to dispose of Vennie can be obtained.

But Miss Betty Pettigru, who has not hesitated in the past to use the power of the blackball or the weapon of the impeachment clause to bully out a victory in Nashville club circles, is truly shocked that Vance had seen she was capable of low tactics and had thought she might "enter into a conspiracy with little children in the house of her kinspeople." She is brought to the realization that women are bound by a more stringent moral order than men:

"Wrong though it seemed, the things a man did to win happiness in the world—or in the only world Miss Betty knew—were of no consequence to the children he came home to at night, but every act, word, and thought of a woman was judged by and reflected in the children, in the husband, in all who loved her." And Miss Betty, for her "new start in life," has chosen the kind of domesticity where a woman's moral decisions matter most. When the final exposure of Vennie comes, Miss Betty has had no direct hand in it.

Miss Betty is not the only one to derive insights from the Vennie episode. Her cousin and companion, the gentle and timid Flo Dear, also reaches an important realization: "It seemed to her that perhaps to do anything at all in the world was to do wrong to *someone*." Her own way of life has been essentially passive and therefore not harmful to others, but she now judges Miss Betty more kindly; for Miss Betty, by the very activeness of her love, seemed bound to hurt someone. Further, though Flo Dear has long been an authority on Tennessee genealogy, she only at this point seems to have sensed the full significance of family love in qualifying moral relationships. At the end of the story, at any rate, Flo Dear is elucidating to the three boys "just exactly what her family connection was with them, and in even greater detail . . . the blood ties that existed between them and their Auntie Bet." And the boys, we are told, listened attentively, "as though they were learning life's most important lessons."

"A Past Era, a Better Era"

What is almost a compendium of such "important lessons" is found in another story of family ties, "Their Losses," the first entry in the volume. A Pullman car on a Southern Railroad train en route westward from Grand Junction, Tennessee, to Memphis is the setting that brings together three Tennessee women who vigorously debate the moral reasons for mourning or not mourning over family deaths. Each of the three has just experienced or is about to experience the death of a close relative. Miss Patty Bean of Thornton is bringing home an aged and mentally ill aunt to spend her last days "where she is greatly loved." Miss Ellen Louise Watkins of Brownsville is escorting her mother's body from Sweetwater, where she died, to Brownsville, where she will be buried. And Mrs. Cornelia Weatherby Werner of Memphis is just returning from Grand Junction where she put her old mother "to her last rest."

The three women's reactions to "their losses" are quite varied. Miss Ellen's attitude is the most conventional; she believes in mourning as the sentimental response that love naturally motivates. Cornelia, on the other hand, refuses to mourn the death of her own mother, who, she says, was "opinionated and narrow and mentally cruel to her children and her husband" and "tied to things that were over and done with before she was born." Cornelia's position is like Miss Ellen's, however, in that she makes the propriety of the mourning depend on the worthiness of the person lost. It is Miss Patty who articulates a purely rationalistic defense of the custom of mourning.

"Mourning is an obligation," Miss Patty tells the others. "We only mourn those with whom we have some real connection, people who have represented something important and fundamental in our lives." She makes it clear that she is not speaking of wearing black—the "symbol" of mourning—but of the mourning itself. "I shall mourn the loss of my aunt when she goes, because she is my aunt, because she is the last of my aunts, and particularly because she is an aunt who has maintained a worthwhile position in the world," she says, insisting that how she regarded the members of her family as individuals is "neither here nor there." My people happened to be very much *of* the world," Miss Patty adds. "Not of *this* world but of *a* world that we have seen disappear. In mourning my family, I mourn that world's disappearance."

That world, of course, is the world of the vanishing towns the train has been passing through. The towns, the three women have agreed, were "good towns," "fine towns," "lovely towns," with "the atmosphere of a prosperous and civilized existence." These towns contrast sharply with a modern metropolis like Memphis, which Miss Patty avers she never liked, which Miss Ellen says never liked her, and which Cornelia, who lives there, admits is a "wretched place," where "they can't forgive you for being from the country." The significance of the small towns is that they—or at least the women in them, Taylor's metaphoric widows—have "wanted to retain the standards of a past era, a better era."

"Not as People but as Symbols"

The remaining two stories in *The Widows of Thornton* also take up cultural contrasts, but represent them in characters of different generations. "Porte-Cochere" presents the antagonistic relationship between an elderly father and one of his sons, and "Bad Dreams" details an equally antagonistic relationship between a young black servant couple and an aged black tramp who intrudes on their domestic privacy. In the first story, we see the circumstances largely through the older person's point of view; in the second, primarily through the young people's.

Old Ben Brantley in "Porte-Cochere" is a crotchety egocentric of seventy-six years who badgers petulantly the five children who come back to Nashville to visit him on his birthday. From his study (opening on the landing halfway between the first and second floors of his house), above the porte-cochere, Old Ben can spy on his children whether they are in the yard, on the side-porch, or in the house; and he can snare their attention to himself any time they use the stairs. In an orgy of self-pity Old Ben thinks: "What would old age be without children? Desolation, desolation. But what would old age be with children who chose to ignore the small demands that he would make upon them, that he had ever made upon them? A nameless torment!" His older son Clifford, whom he particularly harasses, can only wonder at his father's motives and desires: "It's your children that have got old, and you've stayed young—and not in any good sense, Papa, only in a bad one! You play sly games with us still or you quarrel with us. What the hell do you want of us, Papa? I've thought about it a lot. Why haven't you ever asked for what it is you want? Or are *we* all blind and it's really obvious?"

Old Ben's memories of his own childhood supply us with some of the answer. Suffering under the harsh discipline of a cruel father, Ben in his youth had vowed to "go away to another country . . . where there would be no children and no fathers." Wanting his own house "to be as different from his father's house as a house could be," he has given his own children a freedom he had never known but has "tortured and plagued them in all the ways that his resentment of their very good fortune had taught him to do." In a gesture of senile despair and frustration he draws out the very stick (with his father's bearded face carved on it) with which has father used to beat him and flays the chairs of his room while "calling the names of his children under his breath."

In "Bad Dreams" Taylor gives us the equally frustrated desires of youth to protect itself from the demands of old age. Emmaline and Bert, maid and houseboy for the James Tolliver family in St. Louis, are highly resentful when Mr. Tolliver brings a disreputable old Thornton black man to share the servants' quarters with them and their four-month-old nameless baby. Realizing all too well that the old man, once deposited upon them, will be their complete responsibility, Emmaline and Bert make vague plans to "get shed of" the old man. Only when the unsavory old-timer helps them out of a middle-of-the-night crisis with a shrieking and gasping baby—he convinces them the child is not sick but only has "bad dreams"—is an uncertain reconciliation of the two generations effected.

The old man has represented many things to Bert and Emmaline. He is the image of "all the poverty and nigger life" they had escaped when they left Thornton for St. Louis. He is an overt threat to their humble aspirations: to keep their baby with them and to convert the extra servant's room into a nursery. He is a reminder of the humiliations blacks must suffer at the hands of whites. When the old man explains the baby's nightmare—"I reckon he thought the boogyman after him"—he is also explaining Bert and Emmaline's reaction to himself and the dreams from which they had been awakened.

Yet Taylor specifically warns that it may be necessary for us to treat such "pathetic old tramps," who have somehow "moved beyond the reach of human imagination" in their unlikeness to us, "not as people but as symbols of something we like or dislike." Their "loneliness" is both the evidence of their estrangement from humanity and the proof of their kinship with it. This passage at the end of the story—a passage that almost abandons the pretense of a character's point of view and speaks with auctorial directness—ends with a reflection that the old man too may have his "bad dreams" like Bert and Emmaline and the nameless baby. The only comfort is that there certainly will not be so many ahead for him as for the others.

Together the two stories, "Porte-Cochere" and "Bad Dreams," suggest once more the mystery of human personality and the terrible barriers to love and understanding even among those with natural affinities. And in the total context of *The Widows of Thornton* the two stories remind us again of the certain necessity but dubious possibility of trying to preserve those ties—of blood, of love, of history, and of institutions—that alone keep people somehow together even in their loneliness.

Chapter Five

From Fiction to Drama

"The Curtain Rises"

The early stories of Peter Taylor, with their undramatic conflicts, their drawn-out characterizations, their dependence upon nuances of descriptive language for the maintenance of authenticity of setting and delicacy of tone, certainly did not hold out any special promise of playwriting talent. Nevertheless, Taylor was moving steadily toward the new genre. Kenneth Clay Cathey, for one, detected a developing dramatic sense in "Allegiance" (1947) and the stories following it.[1] And between the end of the war and the time *A Long Fourth* was published in 1948 Taylor had reportedly already written two plays. Since then, he has maintained a steady interest in playwriting, which he considers an exercise more natural for the short-story writer than novel-writing.

In the winter of 1949 the first of Taylor's dramatic works to be published, *The Death of a Kinsman,* appeared in *Sewanee Review.*[2] Taylor has revealed that it was originally written as a short story but rewritten as a play because in story form it became "too difficult . . . not to be explicit and literal about the meaning of certain experiences and the psychology of certain characters." "In a play," he says, "because of the blessed limitations of the form, it is at least not so obvious when information is withheld."[3] As we have already seen, *The Death of a Kinsman,* in its single act, develops an interesting variation on the "widowhood" theme which unifies the diverse pieces in *The Widows of Thornton.* In addition, it gives provocative insights into the plight of the transplanted Southerner, into the necessity of role-playing in the achievement of family harmony, and into the multiple and complex relationships that exist between sexes, generations, classes, races, and regions.

As perceptive as it is thematically, the play is nevertheless problematic to produce. One-act plays with a multiethnic cast of twelve are not in great demand—especially when five of the roles are for children ranging in age from four to twelve. More limiting still is the set called for: it must simulate the upstairs hall-sitting room of "one of those mansions put up in Midwestern cities during the early part of the present century," complete with large stair, oak balustrades, pilasters, and elaborate door facings. It is hard to imagine an actual set capable of revealing the subtle distinctions called for in the author's stage directions: "The floor is not carpeted, but it is partly covered by two large rugs. The one on the left is a handsome, though rather worn and faded, Oriental rug. On the right is an obviously new imitation of the same thing, with extremely bright colors and a general effect of silkiness."

The chief question about *The Death of a Kinsman* is whether its artistic point can in fact be realized on stage, since such nuances (which add so much to Taylor's stories) may be difficult if not impossible to convey to a theater audience. Brainard Cheney, considering the possibility that Taylor's plays may only be "fiction . . . in the trappings of plays," concludes that *The Death of a Kinsman* does "*fictional* violence to an axiom of the theater—the maxim that a play must make its points obviously, that it cannot resort to the techniques of indirection practiced in fiction because the spectator has only the passing instant in which to grasp the meaning of the action."[4] Kenneth Clay Cathey calls the play "obviously experimental," but suspects "it is incapable of holding an audience's attention throughout an actual stage performance since the entire first half accomplishes nothing but exposition."[5] Morgan Blum finds an even greater deficiency in "the essentially undramatic quality of its ending"—an ending "based on the kind of self-discovery that is inevitably blurred for many members of a theater audience because it is difficult to find a clearcut way of presenting, on the stage, anything so essentially inward." Blum argues that the device Taylor employs to point up the concluding self-discovery by Aunt Lida (a subtle positioning of the characters as the curtain falls) is "unsatisfactory," since it "does not define the play's change, the degree to which the discovery is accepted, with any real precision"—the way, for instance, looking into the character's consciousness might have done it in a short story.[6]

Of course, theatrical conventions have changed so much in the four decades since *The Death of a Kinsman* first hit the boards that what was once considered only a somewhat rewarding closet drama might well take on surprising new life if resurrected in an attentive professional production today.

"A Microcosm of Life Back Home"

Tennessee Day in St. Louis (1957) repeats a number of the problematic traits of *The Death of a Kinsman,* but it is, by and large, a more satisfactory adjustment to stage conventions.[7] It manages to transfer to the new genre many of the most appealing features of Taylor's short fiction. In the larger expanse of its four acts it is able to bring life to the Tolliver family to a degree that *The Death of a Kinsman* could not quite manage for the Wades. Certainly, the intertwinings of familial relationships are as complex here as in any of the longish short stories of the previous books.

The Tolliver family depicted in the play is the same Tolliver family featured in "Two Ladies in Retirement" and alluded to in "Bad Dreams" and other stories of *The Widows of Thornton*. Several modifications in the Tolliver menage are, however, apparent. The three sons found in "Two Ladies in Retirement" are here reduced to two, Jim and Lanny (called Jimmy and Landon in the earlier work). Though Vance has disappeared, some of his character traits seem to have been taken over by Lanny (who, incidentally, has also taken over the birthday assigned to Jimmy in "Two Ladies in Retirement"). Only one servant, Bert (who was featured in "Bad Dreams"), appears on stage, but the presence of Emmaline and other help in the offstage background is implied and not difficult to imagine. Miss Betty Pettigru (called Auntie Bet here) and Flo Dear, her gentle companion, reveal the same basic character traits they had in "Two Ladies in Retirement." The father of the family, James Tolliver, is likewise consistent with his earlier image. The only character to undergo some significant transformation is the mother, whose name is changed from Amy to Helen and who seems here more ebullient than before.

Several additional kinfolk have been introduced into the Tolliver household for the play. The most important is Helen's brother William, whose antifamilial ideas provide a direct contrast with his environment. On the periphery of the family is William's mistress, Lucy McDougal, who has been given entrée into the intimate family circle under the fiction that she is William's secretary and fiancée. And visiting the Tollivers over Tennessee Day are Helen's distant cousin, Senator Cameron Caswell, and his granddaughter, Nancy. All of these characters are defined not only by their roles in the family but by their attitudes toward their roles.

The events of the play are not outwardly momentous, though Lanny's attempted suicide at the end of act 2 is at least potentially tragic. Various characters merely pass by each other in the different ritual encounters of family living, protected from too-direct confrontations by the social conventions that assign complementary roles to all. Only in the brief moments between ritual activities, when the protective conventions are not fully operative, do repressed tensions and antagonisms break forth in mild personal clashes. Yet such occasions are sufficient in the course of the play's single day to bring out conflicts between Lanny and William, William and Lucy, Lucy and Auntie Bet, Auntie Bet and Senator Caswell, and Senator Caswell and Lanny.

What gives significance to the slight happenings of the plot is the sociocultural context in which they occur. Although the play has its universal values, its action is firmly grounded in a clearly defined interval of historic time and in a clearly specified geographic milieu. The title focuses attention on both time and place: the occasion is Tennessee Day, 8 January 1939; and the locale is St. Louis, Missouri, one of the Midwestern metropolises in which so many of Taylor's old-time Southerners find themselves transplanted but not yet fully acculturated.

Tennessee Day annually celebrates an epic victory by an almost mythic Southerner—the famous Battle of New Orleans in which Andrew Jackson with only six thousand men defeated twelve thousand British troops in 1815. Like many other events of Southern history, the Battle of New Orleans is both incredible and ironic, incredible because Jackson lost only seven men to the British loss of two thousand, ironic because the belated triumph took place two weeks after a peace treaty had been signed. In Peter Taylor's own life Tennessee Day has added significance, for 8 January is both the date on which his parents were married (in 1908) and the date on which he was born (in 1917). In the play, too, Taylor makes Tennessee Day a triple feast as James and Helen's anniversary and Lanny's birthday. It is no doubt symbolic that the celebration of these two familial and personal occasions of the Tollivers is temporarily quashed in deference to Senator Caswell, the high priest of the civic holy day.

Senator Caswell is, in fact, the hierophant who elucidates the mysteries of the ritual occasion. The play opens with the senator rehearsing his Tennessee Day banquet speech and intoning Delphic phrases full of portent and prophecy. As a former poet, lecturer, actor, and literary man, the senator is a professional interpreter of social history who does not hesitate to expound the meaning he sees in present circumstances. "In the midst of the delights which the modern city offers, you have the delights of the old-fashioned country family," Senator Caswell tells James. "You have your Negro servants and your children and your dependent kinfolks all about you here in one house." For him the Tolliver household is "a sort of microcosm of life back home" where "all the familiar patterns, all the cherished paraphernalia" can be enjoyed without the "responsibility" that went with them in the old environment.

Most of the characters fail to take the senator and his pronouncements with much seriousness; their attitudes range from William's contemptuous mockery to James's good-humored tolerance. Only Lanny accepts the senator as seer and prophet. "It is really terribly exciting having him here," Lanny tells Lucy. "It is like having someone out of the distant past step into the present." He adds: "I have thought just seeing him would be the answer to a million questions I have had about who I am and about our whole family." For

Lanny, the senator is the archetypal Southern gentleman—"something you will never see duplicated, never repeated, that there isn't any more of."

"By Any Sensible Reckoning of History"

It is just because the senator has such significance for Lanny that he becomes an important element in the play's main drama—a drama which is played out on the unlikely stage of Lanny's sensitive adolescent consciousness. Ultimately, all the external action of the play is related to the maturation process that takes place in Lanny. Lanny is introduced in act 1 as a mildly precocious, slightly spoiled, and highly imaginative youth who is seeking his identity in the South's mythic past, which the old senator symbolizes. Though he begs the senator to tell him about "the old days back in Tennessee," he is probing for "ideas," not just "stories and anecdotes" like those he hears from his family. The stories may mean something, Lanny admits, but he does not know what it is; the senator does not *have* the answer, Lanny feels, but actually *is* the answer to the riddle of what the stories mean. Lanny has sought answers in history before (his reading ironically includes *The Decline and Fall of the Roman Empire* and a biography of Sam Davis, boy-hero of the Confederacy), but his first exposure to some facts of recent history (the truth about Lucy's relationship to his Uncle William) is so traumatic that it leads to his suicide attempt. Only at the end of the play, when he finally gets his audience with Senator Caswell, does Lanny learn the inadequacy of the past to explain the present.

That climactic revelation occurs in one of the longest speeches of the play, when the senator, who has previously rebuffed Lanny's inquiries, provides him with the "philosophic point" he has been after. The point is couched in a fable that the senator narrates about his own similar search for meaning in the experience of another seer-figure, an ancient black slave, the son of a Congo chieftain. The then-young Cameron Caswell had vicariously lived through old Prince's jungle exploits so vividly that he passionately shared Prince's tribal loyalties, lay awake nights wishing he could have been born to such a life, and had a "senseless longing to go to some faraway place and live the life of the noble savage." The relationship, however, is only partly parallel to the present one between Lanny and the senator, as the senator explains to Lanny:

> But, you know, even as a little fellow I knew somehow that when I held converse with Prince it was not with a man who had been a boy a hundred years back but, as far as I was concerned, a thousand years back, perhaps ten thousand years. That was something self-evident; there was no confusion in our minds about it . . . (*Standing*) But,

> you see, that would not have been so with you and me. I would have talked to you about old times back home as though it was all day before yesterday, as you no doubt believe it was. But it isn't so! By any sensible reckoning of history there are a thousand years between your generation and mine. (*Begins to leave*) Son, a man who was born in 1854 is older than any of the persons assembled in this house tonight has yet dared to dream. And in another decade or two, even such a meeting as that one I addressed tonight—if anyone recalls it—will seem like something out of an age ancient and remote. (*TD,* 158)

That Lanny learns the lesson the senator teaches is shown by the final gesture of the play. Allowed at last to celebrate his birthday, after the departure of the senator, Lanny is hesitating over the candles on his birthday cake, wondering what to wish. Goaded by his parents to blow out the candles before he sets the house on fire, Lanny slowly and hypnotically utters the play's curtain line: "Give me time. Give me time." It is his symbolic abandonment of the mythic past for the ever-burning present.

"Nothing in Common but Games"

Surrounding Lanny throughout the play are the other members of the household who provide parallels with and contrasts to the main action. Each has made or is making some kind of accommodation to the problem Lanny is only now broaching. The senator, of course, made his long ago. So, too, did Auntie Bet and Flo Dear, who learned to play the only "cards" they had to play. James and Helen have adopted the roles of "eternal sweethearts"; "Their motto," William says, "is: Life must *seem* beautiful." Still wavering in their positions are William and Lucy, and Jim and Nancy.

The point of reference for all is the position of James and Helen, the position most like the traditional. By the device of having one character symbolically assume another character's earlier position, Taylor points out the interrelationships between all the positions. At several moments in the play it is made clear that William is a modern parallel to the old senator and that Jim is trying to parallel William. Lucy, moreover, is shown to have the possibility of paralleling either Auntie Bet as a self-willed and independent woman or Helen as an indispensable wife and mother; Nancy hesitates between Lucy's and Helen's footsteps. The last two analogies are helped by the thoroughly theatrical trick of having both Lucy and Nancy borrow Helen's clothes: Nancy, because she needs an old-fashioned dress for a 1920s party; Lucy, because she has to substitute at the last minute (after Lanny's debacle with the sleeping pills) at the Tennessee Society banquet.

The whole of act 3 is little more than a development of Lucy's alternatives. The scene opens with Lucy stopping the pendulum on the mantle clock and ends with her starting it again. In the timeless interval Lucy hears her possibilities outlined by William and Auntie Bet. William, who has been planning to run out on Lucy, first mistakes her in Helen's dress for the wifely Helen; subsequently, he is moved to offer to marry her so that they may offer Lanny a new kind of parental relationship. Then Auntie Bet reveals with merciless candor that the alternative to becoming Helen is becoming a loveless nothing. It is significant that, in act 4, Nancy, who has talked of running away with Jim and/or William, stays behind in Helen's dress, but Lucy "clears out," even tearing Helen's borrowed dress in her haste to get out of it.

Differing attitudes toward the function of a "family" underlie the diverse actions. For William and for Lucy, too, when she was younger, the family represented a "drag" on one's independence that had to be shaken off; thus they set up their unorthodox liaison supposedly without the hated bindings of "human ties." But, as William says, Lucy "matured"; and he did not. "You know, and I know," William tells her, "it was coming here and seeing James and Helen with their boys that changed you. You began to think maybe farms were not the only place families still made sense. Families were not such awful, out-of-date things, after all. You never said those things, but I could tell when you began to think them." Auntie Bet, whose rich father was never able to find her a husband, kept her life from being "a pretty sad and pointless affair" first by learning to live as the men of her generation did, then by giving up her independence to attach herself to her surrogate children, the Tolliver boys. Nancy and Jim at first wish to escape from family life, but, finally, like Lucy seem to have a change of heart.

Ironically, the exemplars of family responsibility, James and Helen, run a menage characterized by luxurious extravagance, complete apathy regarding discipline, and gratuitous indulgence of selves and children. Taylor uses game imagery, which constantly recurs in both the action and the dialogue, to provide ironic commentary on the ceremonial formality that supports the Tollivers' domestic facade. The play opens in the game room with Auntie Bet and Flo Dear working a jigsaw puzzle; it closes in the same room with the whole family playing a guessing game over the birthday and anniversary presents. In between, various characters (usually at the instigation of Helen, the perpetual "organizer" of family games) have engaged in gambling contests, crossword puzzles, solitaire, darts, and keno. Helen at one point admits that the games are a deliberate diversion to avoid unwanted thoughts.[8] "The trouble with Mother and Father," Lanny says, "is that they have nothing in common but games. They have to play games to keep from boring each other to death."

The charm of a game is that, involving as it does both luck and skill, it is (in Senator Caswell's words) "like a small abstraction of life itself—so much so that it seems almost a sacred thing." The long discussion of gambling by the various characters in act 2 provides the clue for understanding Lanny's suicide attempt, which is taking place at that very moment offstage, following his discovery of William and Lucy's relationship. William argues that "gambling doesn't appeal to people . . . who have real self-confidence or to people who know—or think they know—what life is worth to them," but only to nervous, senseless people who only know "that they have nothing and they ought to want something."

The senator, on the other hand, admires the gentleman-gamblers of Andrew Jackson's day who felt that gambling was "good for the soul." He emphasizes the part played by luck even in a political contest: "Campaign all you will, the outcome of an election depends on things too diverse to consider. Everything from the conversion of St. Paul to the defeat of Prince Charlie counts for or against you in one way or another . . . . How these things fall together for you constitutes your luck." William rejects, however, history's importance to the fortunes of an individual: "You can have history. The trick is to operate outside history. The only interest anybody should have in past history should be for the purpose of better exploiting present history." And this, of course, is very close to the insight that comes to Lanny at the end of the play.

With his first two published plays, then, Peter Taylor discovered that some of his favorite themes could come to life in the theatrical medium as well as in short fiction. He would therefore keep experimenting with dramatic forms off and on throughout the rest of his career.

Chapter Six
Happy Families Are All Alike
"About Being an Artist"

Peter Taylor does not fulfill the strange modern expectation that "really serious" creative writers will spend almost as much time explaining the theory and method behind their work as they do in producing that work in the first place. Aside from casual comments in interviews and occasional public tributes to writer friends, Taylor seldom even comes close to indulging in aesthetic theory or criticism and he generally eschews in his fiction the subject of art and artists.

For this reason "1939," the first story Taylor published after *The Widows of Thornton* and the first story in which he takes up the subject of art, gains a special importance in the overall study of his work. In many ways "1939" also marks the beginning of a shift in style and format that becomes evident in nearly all the stories in *Happy Families Are All Alike* (1959), his third collection of fiction.[1] The fact that it deals with the literary aspirations of a young writer much like Peter Taylor in his Kenyon College days helps to provide some clues to the implications of the new direction in his fiction.

The heroes of "1939" are two modern knights-errant on a semimystic quest. That their point of origin is Gambier, Ohio, and their destination New York City does not diminish the significance of their "ride through the dark, wooded countryside of Pennsylvania on that autumn night" over roads that "wound about the great domelike hills of that region and through the deep valleys in a way that answered some need." For, like their medieval counterparts, these two Kenyon College knights are spurred by an ideal. The narrator confides: "At the time—that is, during the dark hours of the drive East—each of us carried in his mind an image of the girl who had inspired him to make their journey." Furthermore, he recognizes that "the two glorious girls" are but the "particular objects" toward which they are being led by their "inner yearnings for mature and adult experience," the quixotic illusion that they pursue.

The background of the two young men is carefully sketched into the story. The narrator and his roommate, Jim Prewitt, are "restless and uneasy" in the doldrums of their senior year (which, of course, was a tense prewar year), and they take off on their Thanksgiving holiday jaunt not even sure (they say) that they will return. What they are leaving behind is Douglass House, an old home converted into a residence for a group of student writers, each of whom transferred to Kenyon in his sophomore year to study under a "famous and distinguished" poet just appointed to the staff of the English department. But the two travelers do not think of themselves as linked in any kind of "fraternity" to their fellow students in Douglass House; rather, all the Douglass House inmates see themselves as "independents" who intend to remain independent.

And what of the modern Glorianas they are seeking in New York City? To the two questing boys, the "two glorious girls" are both actual artists and symbols of all that is good in the artistic way of life. Unfortunately, as many a knight has learned before, appearances can be deceiving. The narrator's girlfriend, Nancy Gibault, turns out to be neither an artist nor a girlfriend; art school has made her see that she is no artist, and a big bourgeois "German oaf" from St. Louis has made her see she cannot be the narrator's girlfriend. In anger and humiliation, the narrator cruelly chides her about her near-mistake "about being an artist," saying he could tell at sight that she was not one. Jim Prewitt's girl, Carol Crawford, on the other hand, is at the other extreme—the extreme of bohemian pretentiousness. Both are lacking in "the talent and the character and the original mind" that the two boys thought they remembered in them; both are as "worldly and as commonplace as could be."

If the two distressing damsels do not provide the noble adventure their cavaliers had expected, they nevertheless are the catalysts for a genuinely "mature and adult experience" that leads to the "complete and permanent disenchantment" of the two boys. The climactic event of the journey occurs on the train back to Kenyon when the aggrieved young men engage in an almost ceremonial unmasking and combat. As each produces the piece of writing he has just made about his New York experience, the other sarcastically exposes it for what it is: in Jim Prewitt's case, a pompous imitation of W. B. Yeats; in the narrator's case, an unconscious parody of Henry James. There then follows, in the smoking car of the train, a semiviolent joust in which they ram each other with shoulder blocks as though in a "game" of football. When they are finally separated by the conductor, the narrator falls into a "blissful" but restless sleep in his coach seat while the train wheels seem to be saying "*Not yet, not yet, not yet.*"

One final incident remains in the story. When the now-reconciled travelers reach their room in Douglass House, they find the seven students they left behind gathered for a one o'clock in the morning snack around the narrator's hot plate on the "little three-legged oak table in the very center of the room." At first outraged, the two boys eventually relax, laugh, and join with the others in what amounts to a symbolic fellowship feast about the fraternal Round Table. The youthful would-be artists have apparently learned one adult truth: artists cannot cut themselves off from their fellows in their search for their ideal. But, as the narrator stands groggily surveying the situation, he finds it hard to believe "that the trip was over"; and, as if in confirmation that it is not, he hears again "the train wheels saying *Not yet, not yet, not yet.*"

"Mature and Adult Experience"

The story "1939" focuses attention on two elements that dominate the stories in *Happy Families Are All Alike.* The first is a thematic motif about the relationship of experience to wisdom. The second is a narrative technique that shapes the action into the form of an autobiographical memoir.

The experience-wisdom theme in "1939" is tied to the problem of the artistic quest. The two Kenyon seniors are convinced as they begin their New York trip that prospective writers have a special responsibility to drink deep of the Pierian spring:

> The two of us were setting out on this trip not in search of the kind of quick success in the world that had so degraded our former friend [who won a publisher's advance and fled Kenyon] in our eyes; we sought, rather, a taste—or foretaste—of "life's deeper and more real experience," the kind that dormitory life seemed to deprive us of. We expressed these yearnings in just those words that I have put in quotation marks, not feeling the need for any show of delicate restraint. We, at twenty, had no abhorrence of raw ideas or explicit statement. We didn't hesitate to say what we wanted to be and what we felt we must have in order to become that. We wanted to be writers, and we knew well enough that before we could write we had to have "mature and adult experience." And, by God, we *said* so to each other, there in the car as we sped through towns like Turtle Creek and Greensburg and Acme. (*HF,* 219–20; *CS,* 336–37)

As the questing pair set off, however, the narrator has a sudden mental glimpse of the Douglass House boys staring after them—but with the disconcerting image of his own face and that of Jim Prewitt among the gaping figures. The implication is that the romantic pursuit of wisdom is a consciously indulged fantasy.

The little-boy type of surly self-sufficiency that the narrator affects is contrasted with a more mature type of independence that his girl Nancy gains for herself. Her new autonomy is revealed in her rejection of "the seedy-looking undergraduate in search of 'mature experience'" who is the narrator. "Nancy had never seen me out of St. Louis before, and since she had seen me last, she had seen Manhattan," the narrator realizes. "To be fair to her, though, she had seen something more important than that. She had, for better or for worse, seen herself." To see one's self, the whole story seems to say, is the first step toward wisdom—for the artist as well as for the rest of the world.

Thus it is of great importance to the success of the story that the action is related "in the form of a memoir" from the perspective of a later time (presumably the mid-fifties). The narrator may not have had great wisdom at the time when he was a participant in the quixotic quest, but somewhere between then and the time of the narration he has learned to see himself. At one point in the story, after a couple of apparently irrelevant anecdotes, the narrator calls attention to his present point of view:

> Probably I seem to be saying too much about things that I understood only long after the event of my story. But the need for the above digression seemed no less urgent to me than did that concerning the former owner of our car. In his case, the digression dealt mostly with events of a slightly earlier time. Here it has dealt with a wisdom acquired at a much later time. And now I find that I am still not quite finished with speaking of that later time and wisdom. Before seeing me again in the car that November night in 1939, picture me for just a moment—much changed in appearance and looking at you through gold-rimmed spectacles—behind the lectern in a classroom. I stand before the class as a kind of journeyman writer, a type of whom Trollope might have approved, but one who has known neither the financial success of the facile Harvard boy nor the reputation of Carol Crawford. Yet this man behind the lectern is a man who seems happy in the knowledge that he knows—or thinks he knows—what he is about. And from behind his lectern he is saying that any story that is written in the form of a memoir should give offense to no one, because before a writer can make a person he has known fit into such a story—or any story, for that matter—he must do more than change the real name of that person. He must inevitably do such violence to that person's character that the so-called original is forever lost to the story. (*HF,* 222; *CS,* 338–39)

This passage makes several points relevant not only to the technique of "1939" but to that of much of Taylor's later work.

In the first place we can observe that the "memoir" form referred to becomes increasingly popular with Taylor in the stories written after 1955. Although *A Woman of Means* was a first-person narrative, only three of the seven stories in *A Long Fourth* were told in the first person, and not one of the stories in *The Widows of Thornton* was. On the other hand, twenty of the thirty-one new stories in his next five collections—plus most of his later uncollected stories—are first-person narratives. Furthermore, in these first-person stories, some major biographical facts about the narrators are frequently closely parallel to those of the author himself.

"1939" probably raises the question of autobiography in Peter Taylor's art as pointedly as any other story. Taylor has said he wrote the story while he was on the faculty at Kenyon after receiving a challenge at a cocktail party to write something about his college days. He has admitted that "it all happened" and that it is "almost literally true."[2] Taylor himself, Robert Lowell, and Jean Stafford were the prototypes of the characters of the narrator, Jim Prewitt, and Carol Crawford, though the Yeatsian poem attributed to Prewitt was in actuality Taylor's, not Lowell's ("Lowell said that if I'd used one of his, he'd have sued me all the way to the Supreme Court"). Morgan Blum, in his study of Taylor's use of the autobiographical as a type of self-limitation, has pointed out some significant ways in which Taylor diverged from autobiographical facts. The point in question, Blum says, is not whether Taylor ever goes beyond the autobiographical (for it is obvious that he does), but "whether he is *ever* autobiographical." Blum concludes that Taylor's fiction is autobiographical only in the sense that it is "always a world he has observed, peopled with folk he has observed," never containing a time, an area, or an activity he could not have in fact observed.[3]

The memoir form of "1939" and similar Taylor stories,then, is only superficially like autobiography. Such stories have a strong basis in the author's personal experience, but that experience is clearly transformed by the shaping vision of the fiction writer.

"Ideas and Truth and Work and People"

Both the experience-wisdom theme and the memoir technique of "1939" can be further elucidated by other stories in *Happy Families Are All Alike.* The experience-wisdom theme, for instance, goes through various permutations in such stories as "Promise of Rain" and "*Je Suis Perdu.*"

"Promise of Rain" is the story of wisdom coming to a seemingly mature man of fifty through an unexpected sharing of the vision of his teenage son. The father, Will Perkins, who is also the narrator of the story, summarizes the experience in the last paragraph:

> . . . I had a strange experience that afternoon. I was fifty, but suddenly I felt very young again. As I wandered through the house I kept thinking of how everything

> must look to Hugh, of what his life was going to be like, and of just what he would be like when he got to be my age. It all seemed very clear to me, and I understood how right it was for him. And because it seemed so clear I realized that the time had come when I could forgive my son the difference there had always been between our two natures. I was fifty, but I had just discovered what it means to see the world through another man's eyes. It is a discovery you are lucky to make at any age, and one that is no less marvelous whether you make it at fifty or fifteen. Because it is only then that the world, as you have seen it through your own eyes, will begin to tell you things about yourself. (*HF,* 68–69; *OF, 115)*

What would be mere sententiousness out of context becomes a vivid truth as the culmination of a series of events in the story.

How has the father been led to his discovery? The story begins with the father's keeping a highly critical watch on his sixteen-year-old son Hugh, who is most often seen preening himself in front of mirrors when at home or wandering aimlessly about when out on the town with his gang of teenage friends. When Hugh develops through a speech class an interest in his own voice, too, and begins recording himself on an old Dictaphone, the father becomes a little worried by what seems to be the growing vanity of his son's life—vanity both in the sense of narcissism and in the sense of futility. So at a loss is the father in understanding his son that he feels as if he and his son drift "though two different cities . . . laid out on the very same tract of land" and occupy "two different houses built upon one piece of ground—houses of identical dimensions and filling one and the same area of cubic space."

Taylor makes clear, however, through the mirror and the Dictaphone imagery, that the boy is only trying to discover himself, to see and hear himself in various roles until he hits upon his true vocation. The father, too, comes to understand this in the crucial incident of the story, the occasion when the boy has a chance to hear himself on radio. The radio station has agreed to carry a public-service program featuring the local speech class only if the regularly scheduled ballgame is rained out that day. Hugh is forced to hope for rain, but the rain that comes and cancels the ballgame also creates such static that the radio program is all but obliterated. The "promise of rain," therefore, is a threat as well. (Several times it is pointed out in the story that Hugh is saving things for a "rainy day.")

On this day of mixed blessings the father, developing an empathy for his son as they wait out the weather, finally manages to sense what his son is seeking and seeing. And, despite the static in the air, the father knows Hugh has found himself in his desire to go into show business—a desire that the sound of his own voice on the radio waves confirms once and for all. Having seen the world through another's eyes for that little moment, the father also sees himself in a new light as part of that world. At fifty, he has at last moved toward an essential new wisdom.

The story "*Je Suis Perdu*" provides another illustration of the experience-wisdom theme, again in a father-child relationship. This time the father is younger—thirty-eight—and the child is a little girl of seven. The setting is Paris on the last day of the father's one-year research leave in that city; the father has finished the work that he had hoped to get done on a book, and the family is packing to return to America. In the course of this day's events the father passes through various moods that culminate in an intellectual revelation.

Though the story is divided into two titled sections, "*L'Allegro*" and "*Il Penseroso,*" it is more than a Miltonic mood piece. "*Je Suis Perdu*" succeeds because it not only graphically represents complex emotional states but also because it lets us see a character taking an important step toward the philosophic serenity that only genuine maturity can produce. The father begins his day hearing the sound of laughter: the domestic merriment of his wife, their baby son, and their little girl. The mirth is contagious, and the father dwells on all the lucky breaks and happy events of the sabbatical year. The mood is broken only temporarily when the excited little girl accidentally overturns a glass of milk, is scolded by her parents, and trembles out her apology in her newly learned French: "*Je regrette. Je regrette.*" The father then thinks of another recent incident when he had heard another pitiable French cry from his daughter momentarily lost in a movie theater: "*Je suis perdue! Je suis perdue!*"

The memory of this lamentation lingers with the father as he goes for a walk in the Luxembourg Gardens. The despairing cry becomes his own in a way that he cannot at first understand. Looking about him for something outside himself that could have crushed his earlier fine spirits, he at last senses that the melancholy, both loathed and divine, comes from within himself:

> It sprang from the same thing his earlier cheerful mood had come from—his own consciousness of how well everything had gone for him this year, and last year, and always, really. It was precisely this, he told himself, that depressed him . . . . Generally speaking, he didn't dislike being himself or being American, but to recognize that he was so definitely . . . the combination he was, and that certain experiences and accomplishments were now typical of him was to recognize how he was getting along in the world and how the time was moving by. He was only thirty-eight. But the bad thought was that he was no longer *going to be* this or that. He *was*. It was a matter of

*be*ing. And to *be* meant, or seemed to mean at such a moment, to *be over with.* (*HF,* 262–63; *CS,* 497)

While he recognizes the thought as literary and platitudinous, he is still under its power until he meets his children and their French maid in the park.

The little girl, with her bright blue eyes, is all that is needed to dispel his dark mood. The public buildings are monstrous and tomblike, the park itself is like a formal cemetery, everything about him seems "finished and over with," and his own future life appears "anticlimactic," until the little girl with her "mysterious power" interrupts the mood of despondency. At that point, he realizes that the pensive melancholy will no longer have the hold over him it has had in the past, that he has reached the point where (in Milton's words) "old experience" has attained "to something like prophetic strain." He knows he has gotten to Paris too late to be much affected by his experience (the way, for instance, his little daughter is affected even in her language), but he also knows that what he has already become is also worthwhile. He may be bound now by his own established habits and the claims of others, but he can admit that "there were ideas and truths and work and people that he loved better even than himself."

"Written in the Form of a Memoir"

"Promise of Rain" is a first-person narrative, "*Je Suis Perdu*" a third-person account. Like most other stories in *Happy Families Are All Alike,* they share many qualities of the memoir form alluded to in "1939," despite their variation in point of view. Although the memoir-type story is most likely to be a first-person account, not every first-person tale is in memoir form. An obvious example is the little oddity "A Walled Garden," which Taylor picked up for *Happy Families* after twice passing it up when making his earlier collections.

"A Walled Garden" is certainly first-person in point of view, but it is as far removed from memoir stories like "1939" and "Promise of Rain" as it is possible to be. The form here is rather that of the dramatic monologue of Browning and Tennyson; the story reads, in fact, like a prose parody of Browning's "My Last Duchess." The speaker is a Memphis matron as ruthless and proud as Browning's Duke of Ferrara; her victim is her own daughter, whose behavior, like that of the Duchess, was unpleasing to the speaker. The audience in this case is a young gentleman caller interested in the daughter. The mother, amidst objective appraisals of the flowers in her garden, reminiscent of the Duke's comments on his art collection, gradually reveals to the young man

how she has created the magnificent formal garden out of her daughter's former playground. The walled garden, then, becomes a rather obvious symbol for the prison the mother has built about the spirit of the girl.

When first published as "Like the Sad Heart of Ruth" in 1941, "A Walled Garden" might have been excused as a kind of technical experiment that a young writer needed to attempt. Taylor has said, however, that the Freudian overtones of the story did not occur to him as he was writing it, although he could see them after students in a friend's college class pointed them out.[4] One critic has noted "a tightness of structure and an avoidance of digressions which actually seem to threaten the artistic value of the work"; another finds its technical skill a "source of real delight," but avers that "if it were the only thing of Mr. Taylor's I had read, I cannot believe I would have gone to any trouble to know more of the author or his remaining writings."[5] In *Happy Families* "A Walled Garden" probably seems even less impressive by comparison to the more leisurely memoir stories that are Taylor's forte.

If the first-person point of view alone is not enough to make a memoir story, what, then, is necessary? A couple of the more effective stories of this type, "A Friend and Protector" and "The Little Cousins," will illustrate the features that are usually dominant. Both of these stories, first of all, are characterized by a simplicity of style that is highly deceptive. The style is not so much conversational or oratorical or mythic, as the style of Welty or Faulkner of McCullers sometimes is, as it is quasi-journalistic, as, for instance, Robert Penn Warren's is in *All the King's Men*. It is almost as if the narrator is writing one of those popular newspaper columns that indulges in folksy reminiscence. We may cite, for example, the opening lines of "A Friend and Protector" and then of "The Little Cousins":

> Family friends would always say how devoted Jesse Munroe was to my uncle. And Jesse himself would tell me sometimes what he would do to anybody who harmed a hair on "that white gentleman's head." . . . While he was telling me the things he would do, I'd often burst out laughing at the very thought of my uncle's baldness. (*HF,* 113; *OF,* 142)

> To the annual Veiled Prophet's Ball children were not cordially invited. High up in the balcony, along with servants and poor relations, they were tolerated . . . . But generally speaking, children were expected to enjoy the Prophet's parade the night before and be content to go to bed without complaint on the night of the Ball. This was twenty-five years ago, of course. There is no telling what the practices are out there in St. Louis now. Children have it much better everywhere nowadays. Perhaps they flock to the Veiled Prophet's Ball by the hundred, and even go to the Statler Hotel for breakfast afterward. (*HF,* 148; *OF,* 181)

The tone is familiar but not really personalized, friendly but not intimate, subjective but not very confidential. It neither promises nor delivers anything that might not be publicly discussed in print if the account were real autobiography rather than fiction.

What is more important, the memoir story is retrospective. The main events are never in the immediate present, but are far enough removed in time to be viewed somewhat dispassionately and, perhaps, with an understanding derived from that perspective in time. In both "A Friend and Protector" and "The Little Cousins" we get the impression that the narrator is a man at least in his thirties, but in the one story he is harking back to some events in his late teens and in the other to an episode when he was nine years old. The emphasis in the stories, then, is not what it would have been if the telling had been closer to the event.

Chronology is not even very important in the typical memoir story. The narrator usually feels free to range backward and forward from the time of the principal event (if there is one), with momentary stops at any attractive spot on the temporal spectrum. The transitional words in a single paragraph of "A Friend and Protector" illustrate the pattern: "Usually . . . . And besides by the time I came along . . . . There had been a number of years when . . . . Then, after this phase . . . ." Habitual action receives at least as much stress in this kind of story as the unusual and dramatic kind.

As a result of the de-emphasizing of temporal sequence, the memoir story hardly seems to have a plot in any conventional sense. Its structure appears as loosely anecdotal as, say, a *Reader's Digest* sketch on "The Most Unforgettable Character I Ever Met." A look at the climaxes in "A Friend and Protector" and "The Little Cousins" shows, however, that the apparent plotlessness is an illusion. In the former story the narrator looks back on the relationships between his uncle and aunt and their black handyman, Jesse Munroe. The narrator recalls (though not in sequential order) how Jesse, while back in the country town of Braxton, Tennessee, had "received a suspended sentence for an alleged part in the murder of Aunt Margaret's washwoman's husband," how Uncle Andrew arranged with the judge to bring Jesse with him and Aunt Margaret when they moved to Memphis, how Jesse began to go on escapades and get into scrapes to counteract the "country boy" teasing he got from the other servants, how Uncle Andrew would always get him out of his jams, and how Jesse's drinking and wild (even criminal) ways grew successively worse. Finally, Jesse goes on a drunken rampage in which he wrecks and ravages Uncle Andrew's office. This time, barricading himself in the ruined office, he calls not for Uncle Andrew but for Aunt Margaret.

When the old woman faces Jesse through the glass door of the office, the narrator suddenly senses the truth about the "protective" relationship he has witnessed over the years:

While she remained there her behavior was such that it made me understand for the first time that this was not merely the story of that purplish-black, kinky-headed Jesse's ruined life. It is the story of my aunt's pathetically unruined life, and my uncle's too, and even my own. I mean to say that at this moment I understood that Jesse's outside activities had been not only *his,* but *ours* too. My Uncle Andrew, with his double standard or triple standard—whichever it was—had most certainly forced Jesse's destruction upon him, and Aunt Margaret had made the complete destruction possible and desirable to him with her censorious words and looks. But they did it because they had to, because they were so dissatisfied with the pale *un*ruin of their own lives. They did it because something would not let them ruin their own lives as they wanted and felt a need to do—as I have often felt a need to do, myself. As who does not sometimes feel a need to do? Without knowing it, I think, Aunt Margaret wanted to see Jesse as he was that morning. (*HF,* 136; *OF,* 160)

This stunning climax, which reverses ironically all the relationships the rest of the story has established, is followed by an anticlimax that is in some ways even more startling. For the narrator finds that Aunt Margaret, far from suffering as he had supposed from a lasting shock, shows no permanent awareness of her role as Jesse's Judas.

In "The Little Cousins" the reminiscences also build up to a nonspectacular but moving denouement. The narrator, recalling his motherless boyhood and the childish sufferings that only his sister Corinna could share and name for him, concludes with what appeared to outsiders as a trivial incident. But the incident is again a betrayal—not a socially destructive one as in "A Friend and Protector," but just as heartrending to the nine-year-old boy. For years the boy has relied on the silent pact that binds his sister to him as companion, confidante, and comforter. The strength of the alliance has been a common enemy, Mary Elizabeth Caswell, an older girl, also motherless, who is held up as a paragon of virtue to the two children. At the story's end the boy finds his sister—overwhelmed by Mary Elizabeth Caswell's glamour and graciousness as Queen of the Veiled Prophet's court—capitulating to the enemy in overtures of friendship. Most devastating of all is the fact that Corinna shares with Mary Elizabeth a special secret that was not hers alone but her brother's as well. So crushed is the little boy by this unexpected abandonment that he bursts into tears that he cannot explain to the solicitously inquiring adults about him.

The memoir story, then, is different from the nonfictional personal history in the way that any work of imaginative literature is different from the literal reproduction of mere facts: it is the product of a carefully controlled design imposed upon the chaos of life in such a way as to reveal transcendent meaning. "Fiction says, 'life is not just chaos: It means something,'" Taylor has said. "You're trying to see sense in events, and you also see how the way things go influences character . . . . That's the reason one can go on writing—to make these discoveries about the past and the present."[6]

Memories, Manners, and Realism

Peter Taylor's memory for the acutely perceived details of social situations is the sustaining force for all the stories in *Happy Families Are All Alike,* both those that are written in memoir form and those that are not. What Katherine Anne Porter once said of herself—that the "exercise of memory" was the "chief occupation" of her mind—might equally well be applied to Taylor. "All my experience seems to be simply memory, with continuity, marginal notes, constant revision and comparison of one thing to another," Porter has said. "Now and again thousands of memories converge, harmonize, arrange themselves around a central idea in a coherent form, and I write a story."[7]

The result of such a convergence of memories in Taylor's work is a close-webbed texture of social realism in the narrative background—as in the story "Guests," one of the most successful in the 1959 collection. Taylor has said that the first two lines of the story ("The house was not itself. Relatives were visiting from the country") were written "without any notion of a plot to follow them." Rediscovered by their author five years later, the same lines inspired a new convergence of memories and imagination, and "the story of a do-gooder wife who insists on importing visitors popped into place."[8]

In "Guests," as in many other Taylor stories, the social realism seems to be a compound of three distinct elements: the authentic reproduction of lifelike details in setting, character description, and dialogue; the distillation of an entire code of manners (or, in this instance, two different codes of manners) into the dramatic conflicts of the plot; and a clear reflection of the psychological reactions occasioned by the code or codes of manners in the particular context.

The first element is readily apparent in "Guests," noticeable especially in the details that contrast the old country couple, Cousin Johnny and Cousin Annie Kincaid, with their big-city host and hostess, Edmund and Henrietta Harper. Cousin Johnny's high-topped shoe, his lisle sock held up by an elastic supporter, and his long underwear showing above the sock are part of this authentic representation of life, but so too is Henrietta's stylish dress with the

mysterious buttons—"so unnecessary, so numerous and so large"—that are carefully camouflaged by being covered with the same print material the dress is made of. This same kind of realism is found in the perfectly rendered conversations: Edmund trying to be unperturbed when Henrietta's phone call interrupts a conference with his law partner and his most important client, or Cousin Annie trying to make a point about how her husband should be addressed (she prefers the "old-fashioned country genteel" form of "Mr. Kincaid") while she is actually talking about his distaste for meat.

The second kind of realism—the re-creation of the intricate behavioral patterns of characters from the different social groups—merges neatly with the realism of physical surface. (It is only the fact that literary history has produced many Arnold Bennetts but only a few Jane Austens that makes it desirable to keep a theoretical distinction between the two types.) Certainly, "Guests" uses surface detail to suggest the different codes of manners of the hosts and the guests: the picture, for instance, of the old country people "seated side by side on the porch swing—rigid as two pieces of graveyard statuary," all packed and fully dressed, their hats on their heads and their house stoutly locked, waiting for their hosts to pick them up.

But in this story Taylor has used an even more emphatic means of calling attention to the comedy of manners he is writing; he has filled the story with the imagery of battle, so that the conflict between Cousin Annie's code and Henrietta's becomes hilariously (and, perhaps also, pathetically) clear. Henrietta is determined that her guests shall have their good attended to, their best interests served, willy-nilly; Cousin Annie is equally determined that they shall endure the outrages of Henrietta's good works without Henrietta's even knowing when or how she offends them. The battle lines are drawn in the opening paragraph:

> Cousin Johnny was on a strict diet. Yet wanting to be no trouble, both he and Cousin Annie refused to reveal any principle of his diet. If he couldn't eat what was being served, he would do without. They made their own beds, washed out their own tubs, avoided using salad forks and butter knives. Upon arriving, they even produced their own old-fashioned ivory napkin rings, and when either of them chanced to spill something on the table cloth, they begged the nearest Negro servant's pardon. As a result, everybody, including the servants, was very uncomfortable from the moment the old couple entered the house. (*HF,* 170–71; *CS,* 407)

At first Edmund thinks Cousin Annie is "waging a merely defensive war against Henrietta," but gradually he sees that she has had "the offensive from the beginning" and even wins the final "victory" when Cousin

Johnny dies in the guest bedroom without his hosts ever knowing for sure that he had been ill.[9]

Manners are especially important in the quiet world that Taylor creates because it is manners that his characters respond to in the moments of heightened perception when they see something anew or for the first time. Thus, in "Guests" what Edmund comes to recognize beneath the social differences is a basic similarity between himself and Cousin Johnny. At first he finds a part of himself "always reaching out and wanting to communicate" with the country guests and another part "forever holding back, as though afraid of what *would* be communicated." Later, "in a flight of fancy that was utterly novel to him," he visualizes how he himself might have been only a country lawyer and Cousin Johnny might have been a shoe company president if each had followed an earlier opportunity.

And, finally, in a silent soliloquy before Cousin Johnny's corpse, he notes that what they had in common was "being from the country," though each had been in some way dissatisfied and responded to the dissatisfaction in his own way: "By 'country' we mean the old world, don't we, Cousin Johnny—the old ways, the old life, where people had real grandfathers and real children, and where love was something that could endure the light of day—something real, not merely a hand one holds in the dark so that sleep will come. Our trouble was, Cousin Johnny, we were lost without our old realities. We couldn't discover what it is people keep alive for without them." The realistic psychological resolution of the story comes naturally, then, from the physical and social realism already established.

Since what appears to be the reality is not always what actually is the reality, a story like "Guests" abounds in little ironies. Thus, Henrietta, who has seemed to be the overwhelming power in the story, winds up vanquished at the hands of her seemingly docile antagonist; and Edmund, who had always accepted Henrietta's contention that she was "more sensitive to people" than he was, turns out to be the only one who senses the full truth of the situation in which they are involved. Although Taylor limits the story to Edmund's point of view, he is still able to unmask fundamental reality by rending its disguises.

In a story like "Heads of Houses," where several points of view are alternately taken up, Taylor is able to multiply a situation's ironies. Perhaps the funniest story Taylor has ever written, "Heads of Houses" is also one of the most serious in theme. Here the three levels of realism are each filtered through three different consciousnesses, so that one viewpoint complements and corrects another.[10]

The subject of "Heads of Houses" is one of those domestic dilemmas that

city that "Promise of Rain" gives, both convey graphic impressions of the ideas and attitudes of the moneyed class during the years of the Great Depression. Chatham seems of a piece with the St. Louis, Detroit, and Chicago of numerous other Taylor works.

Probably the chief contrast between the two stories is one of mood. "Can anyone honestly like having a high-school civics teacher for an uncle?" the narrator asks in the opening sentence of "The Other Times." The first few paragraphs set up an expectation that this will be another leisurely exploration of familial relationships on the order of "The Scoutmaster" or "A Wife of Nashville." On the whole, the story does not disappoint this expectation, but it is hardly one of Taylor's most memorable stories. It probes, satisfactorily enough, the mysterious bonds of family love that link a young girl to her uncle in a way in which she will never be linked to the narrator, her high-school beau.

The plot has a trio of senior boys taking their predeb dates away from a society party and to a speakeasy roadhouse in a neighboring town. There the narrator and the girl Letitia discover her ne'er-do-well uncle, the civics teacher and baseball coach at Chatham's Westside High School, carousing with some of his athletes and their girlfriends. When the place is raided by the authorities, it is Uncle Louis who, after helping hide Letitia and her friends, gallantly sacrifices himself to the humiliation of public arrest (and to the consequent loss of his job). The story ends with the narrator, whose rarefied snobbery pervades the whole account, puzzling over the delicate familial trust that united Letitia with her uncle.

Simple technically but complex thematically, "The Other Times" is a study of the tenuous survival of older patterns in a new cultural climate. Its whole method is understatement: understated characters, understated action, understated themes. "Venus, Cupid, Folly, and Time," on the other hand, is one of the few stories in which Taylor abandons his characteristic method of understatement and deliberately distorts his material for a surrealistic shock effect.

The unusual Gothic mood of "Venus, Cupid, Folly, and Time" begins with the first sentence: "Their house alone would not have made you think there was anything so awfully wrong with Mr. Dorset or his old maid sister." The "dilapidated and curiously mutilated" house would not make us think there was anything "so awfully wrong," that is, as long as we had not already read Faulkner's "A Rose for Emily," Welty's "Clytie," McCullers's "The Ballad of the Sad Café," Capote's *Other Voices, Other Rooms,* or a hundred and one other contemporary Southern stories with decadent houses for even more decadent people. When the house is even more fully described a couple of pages later (it has the third story "torn away" and looks "raw and naked" from the "scars" where a wing was pulled down), the reader should be convinced that something is "awfully wrong" with Peter Taylor's usual style.

The Dorsets are the most grotesque caricatures Taylor has indulged himself with since Mr. Speed in "A Spinster's Tale." We are asked to believe that they are ancient recluses who emerge from their house only three times each year—once to sell artificial flowers (like "sprays of tinted potato chips"), which Miss Dorset makes; once to peddle the withered figs off the family tree; and once (yes, Taylor insists on this, too) to gather up all the pubescent thirteen- and fourteen-year-olds in socially prominent West Vesey Place for a bizarre dancing party at their house. The story centers on the narrator's account of one of these parties, one where two of the invited children smuggle in an intruder and play a crude trick on the aged host and hostess.

Perhaps in deference to possible reader incredulity, Taylor keeps the narrator distant from the main action, which he must reconstruct from the half-legendary accounts of others, filling in the details from other related memories of his own. So merged is the description of the one crucial party where the trick is played with the recollections of parties of other years that the reader is inclined to accept the narrator's statement that "nothing about the one evening when you were actually there ever seemed quite as real as the glimpses and snatches which you got from those people before and after you—the second-hand impressions of the Dorsets' behavior, of things they said, of looks that passed between them." Even when the events of the climactic occasion have been outlined, the narrator offers little help in interpretation:

> But a clear picture of the whole evening wasn't to be had—not without considerable searching. For one thing, the Meriwether parents immediately, within a week after the party, packed their son and daughter off to boarding schools. Accounts from the other children were contradictory and vague—perversely so, it seemed. Parents reported to each other that the little girls had nightmares which were worse even than those which their older sisters had had. And the boys were secretive and elusive, even with us older boys when we questioned them about what had gone on. (*HF,* 94; *CS,* 311–12)

Is the story just a richly suggestive oneiric fantasy? Or is the story, like the color print of Bronzino's *Venus, Cupid, Folly, and Time* that hangs on the landing of the Dorsets' basement stair, deserving of the subtitle "An Allegory"? Taylor has described in interviews how he began the story with a clear synopsis in mind, how he worked it out like a theorem, and how he spent months constructing it as a complete allegory about familial and cultural incest. There are constant insinuations in the story, of course, that aberrant sexuality plays a part in the peculiar actions of the Dorsets. But Taylor applies the incest motif to all the young people, too. "It's a form of incest to want to marry only in your own class, your own background exactly," he has said. "That was the world I had grown up in. I had seen my brother and sisters in it. And some of those young people—it was very sad—*couldn't* marry anyone but that way, and never married because there was nobody in that set for them . . . ; it had to be 'in the family,' so to speak. It *is* a sort of incest to marry within a class, especially when it's within a class in a certain town."[12]

The story is too richly suggestive to be easily limited to a single interpretation, however, and there are ample hints to support other layers of allegory. The Dorsets, for instance, despite their eccentricities, are the "social arbiters" of the city whose ludicrous demands must be submitted to even by "sensible parents" who might wish to reject them. Are they then figures in a fable about the decline of genteel society? But the Dorsets also seem to visualize themselves (as they move about the erotic artwork, slightly hidden and subtly lighted, in the niches and dark corners of their house) as prophets of love, youth, beauty, and sacrifice. "We have given up everything for each other," Miss Dorset says at one time, and adds at another: "This is what it is like to be young forever."[13]

"Venus, Cupid, Folly, and Time" is, no doubt, as the judges for the O. Henry and Martha Foley best-short-story annuals discerned, a tour de force, a genuine success of a kind, a worthy contribution to the modern Southern literature of the grotesque. "The Other Times" is only a straightforward realistic chronicle without noticeable distortion for suggestive effect.[14] But "The Other Times" is typical Peter Taylor, the sort he has described as having "not a word that's made up" and having a tone that "pretended to be just memoirs of genteel families"; and "Venus, Cupid, Folly, and Time" represents a change that he would occasionally (but only occasionally) indulge in some of his future writing, a change toward "made up" stories with carefully contrived plots.[15]

Chapter Seven

Miss Leonora and *Collected Stories*

The Old and the New Together

Peter Taylor's next two volumes after *Happy Families Are All Alike* are both retrospective collections, bringing together some new stories with some old ones from earlier out-of-print volumes. Some of the old stories take on new interest in a changed context, and some of the new stories stretch somewhat the familiar domain of Taylor's fiction.

Miss Leonora When Last Seen (1963) includes six new stories, plus ten pieces from his two Harcourt, Brace collections—four stories from *A Long Fourth* and five stories and the one-act play from *The Widows of Thornton.* But Taylor's relations with the publisher of *Happy Families* and *Miss Leonora* were not harmonious, and the publisher did not keep these two works long in print. Consequently, just a few years later, Taylor moved to a new publisher and there created a new volume, *Collected Stories* (1969), which selected five new tales, two stories from *A Long Fourth* and four from *The Widows of Thornton* (all six of which had also been included in *Miss Leonora*), six from *Happy Families,* and four of the six new stories first collected in *Miss Leonora.*

Despite Taylor's own feeling that his writing underwent a major change of direction after "Venus, Cupid, Folly, and Time," the new stories first assembled in *Miss Leonora* and *Collected Stories* would probably strike the reader as only relatively slight variations on themes and techniques he had already successfully explored. The two stories with which *Miss Leonora* opens, for instance, provide contrasting examples of the kinds of minor forays Taylor is willing to make into new territory. Both "Reservations: A Love Story" and "An Overwhelming Question" deal with young lovers: the first, with a couple on their wedding day; the second, with a couple in the three days before their scheduled wedding. The subject itself, then, was something relatively unusual for Taylor, for the nuptial period was the one phase of family life he had hardly touched on since "Rain in the Heart" in 1945.

"Reservations," based on a funny anecdote Taylor heard in Memphis, introduces us to a bride and groom, Franny and Miles, just as they are making their furtive getaway from the lavish wedding reception and supper dance under way at the country club. Trying to elude their prankster friends and to slip off on their honeymoon unobserved, the newlyweds are forced by a snowstorm to spend their wedding night in town. During some comic misadventures as they make their way to their hotel room, Taylor very ably portrays the alternating surges of anxiety and of bliss that sweep over Fanny. These shifts in mood are nothing, however, compared to the drastic changes Fanny undergoes when, at the climax of the story, she accidentally locks herself in the bathroom.

The bathroom crisis presents the young couple with more than a problem in locksmithery; the unbudging door is a symbol of all the barriers still between them. Taylor has so contrived the situation, too, that Franny and Miles must open the door between them—both the literal and the figurative one—without calling on the usual sources of aid. For the hotel where they are staying is the very hotel where Miles has been living for the last year and a half—the only hotel in the convention-filled city where they were able to get reservations at the last minute when their other plans were derailed by snow. Franny is adamant that Miles shall not call on the hotel employees for help, since the assistant hotel manager is a friend who would not be likely to keep the story of their embarrassment to himself. Miles thus must work on the hinges with jackknife and bottle opener while Franny jiggles the knob.

In the meantime, Franny, in her frustration, and Miles, in his irritation, begin to raise their voices, to exchange accusations and insults, and to hurt and humiliate each other. All the buried grievances are disinterred—Miles's dallyings with other girls, Franny's family's probing into Miles's background—until Franny threatens to drown herself in the bathtub and Miles threatens to jump out the eighth-floor window if she does. The deus ex machina is a mortifying one: a middle-aged prostitute in the next room gets her gentleman to extricate Franny through an adjoining door. The rescuer, Franny suspects, is ironically none other than the assistant hotel manager they had been trying to avoid! The crisis past, the young lovers are "glad they had said all the things . . . through the door," confident in their own "bliss and happiness" that "neither of them would ever deceive or mistrust the other again," now that all the "reservations" in their relationship were canceled. Though Taylor's tone ironically qualifies the optimism expressed, there at least seems little danger of Franny's earlier despairing vision ("of her dear Miles and her dear self lying dead in their caskets with their love yet unfulfilled") coming true.

The second story, "An Overwhelming Question," is also about a misunderstanding between lovers. The comic situation seems promising enough. Isabel Havens is determined to seduce her fiancé, Rudy Banks, in the three days remaining before their wedding. Her rationale is hilarious: "She *would not* serve his purpose. She would not allow him to keep the resolution made by another Rudy Banks. She would not, on their wedding night, be there merely as his idealized something or other." Rudy, though quite a playboy with other women, is just as determined to preserve his "idealized something or other" for his wedding night and so tries to elude Isabel's wiles.

If Taylor in this story relies on the surest suspense plot ever invented, he reserves to himself the right to spring surprises in the denouement. The reader may not know at once just what Taylor is up to, but he should be able to sense at once that "An Overwhelming Question" is a far remove in style and tone from "Reservations." Whereas in "Reservations" the point of view is fairly well restricted to what the young couple sees and feels, either separately or jointly, the point of view in the second story is more objective, with the author commenting directly on his characters as "solemn," for instance, or "comical." Moreover, though there are many realistic observations, in the typical Taylor style, about the manners and mores of the Hunt and Polo Club set, both the central characters and their absurd maneuverings appear amusing but artificial. Franny and Miles seem credible people in a real-life plight; Isabel and Rudy seem highly entertaining characters in a quaint little farce.

But is farce really the explanation? The surprise ending suggests otherwise. Rudy, fleeing again from Isabel's advances, runs out of the clubhouse, through mud and muck, and onto a junkpile of construction materials, where he slips and falls. "It would be many hours before they found him there, and meanwhile the stars shone on his uncovered head and on the muddy soles of his dress slippers," the impersonal narrator intones. "His neck was broken, the life gone out of his body, but he was safe from Isabel at last, poor fellow."

Although the popularity of the so-called black humorists in the sixties made such a resolution to comic complications familiar to most readers, there was little preceding the denouement to suggest that Taylor was attempting black humor here; the tone, while it is not just his usual understated irony, is not quite that of a Terry Southern or a Joseph Heller. Isabel and Rudy, of course, could be mere abstractions in some allegory about the battle of the sexes, but the details of the story certainly don't force such an interpretation.

Both "Reservations" and "An Overwhelming Question" seem to have been playful exercises, stretching just a bit the usual boundaries of a Taylor story. Taylor admits that in "Reservations" he invented "in a spirit of fun" all sorts of

Freudian and phallic symbols ("things that were unprintable in those days, with ungenteel suggestions") that he "completely buried" in the story—so much so that they seemed to have escaped the *New Yorker,* which first published the story, the French women's magazine that reprinted it with lavish illustrations, and the United States Steel Hour, which produced a TV adaptation of it. "By this time I felt rather low," Taylor says, "and I began to imagine that perhaps I had sold out, that I might only have imagined that it was a sexy story, and then I got a lovely letter from Randall Jarrell analyzing the story in the greatest detail and having caught every possible suggestion in it."[1] Perhaps "An Overwhelming Question," too, only needs a reader of Jarrell's sensibility to disinter its jocular meaning.

"A Kind of Knowledge"

Some of Taylor's new stories in *Miss Leonora* plumb just a little deeper than before the ever-intriguing mysteries of human personality, of social interrelationships, and of time and change. The title "A Strange Story," which Taylor appends to one of these new efforts, forewarns that just such a mystery will be found at the heart of the narrative.

"A Strange Story" is a first-person account by a middle-aged protagonist of the enigmatic "voices" that plagued him as a little boy. "How are they to be explained, the voices one heard as a child?" the narrator asks in the first line of the story. He recalls instance after instance when he distinctly heard "voices that came out of the air, from the trunks of trees, and even sometimes out of the mouths of small animals." "You are the Lost Dauphin," the voices might say, or "Good morning to you, Bonaparte." Their messages range from the philosophic to the nonsensical: "Time passes. You haven't got forever"; "Are you going to sit on that Christmas tree all day?"; "There is no one god. And there was no beginning and there will be no end"; and "Oh, ouch, oh, ouch, ouch, ouch!" The narrator rejects categorically the explanation that he was either an "abnormal child" or a "mystic"; he insists instead that the voices he has heard are heard by all children until they are formally forsworn and replaced by the voices of other people. The narrator is different from others only in that he made the mistake of speaking "frankly" on the subject and embarrassing others, who would react not in "disbelief" but in "disgust" at the breach of good taste.

Mixed with the madcap history of the voices is a realistic reminiscence about growing up. The crucial incident here is a dancing-class party where the narrator's date is stolen by his older brother. The two stories merge when, in his distress over the events at the party, the narrator repudiates his pestiferous voices and vows, "I will stop hearing you, you demons who persecute innocent children." From that point on, his task is "learning to listen to the voices of people—still discovering just how carefully, for love's sake, one must always listen."

This half-fantastic, half-humorous parable has something more than half-serious to say about human sensibility and human intuition at different stages of maturity. If we are not born trailing Wordsworthian clouds of glory, we may nevertheless be in closer contact with the numinous forces of nature as children than we are as adults. The unexplained "mystery" of the voices becomes "a kind of knowledge" that "instructs and informs us about the arbitrary nature of most of the things we have to learn in order to walk the world as adults." Told that he cannot be an artist unless he learns to "love Nature," the narrator eventually learns that "strange and wonderful" feat—but he remains ever aware of a childlike relationship to Nature that was closer even than love and that could have made his whole life "different" if he had only pursued his inclination to go on "listening always" to his mysterious voices.

Mystery pervades adult life also, however, as another story in *Miss Leonora,* "Two Pilgrims," amply demonstrates. In this seemingly artless story, a seventeen-year-old boy tells of a trip he made from Memphis to a small town in northern Alabama as a chauffeur for his uncle, a cotton broker, and for his uncle's old friend, a lawyer. On the trip the two older men discuss old times in the country they are passing through—"how good the bird hunting used to be" and the "fine people they knew who had once lived there." Their reminiscing is interrupted when in the old Natchez Trace section they spy a farmhouse on fire. Immediately, they order the boy to stop at the farmhouse and they rush in—with coats pulled over their heads "like a couple of hooded night riders"—to try to save the belongings in the house.

What is peculiar about the situation is the behavior of the farm couple who idly watch the rescue operations. The woman is first alarmed by what she takes for bandits, then bemused that strangers would become "right active" in rescuing "junk" she "heired" from her grandma, and only at length concerned that her child might be in the burning house. Her husband, who had actually had the child with him in the barn, seems equally detached about the loss of possessions and only mutters imprecations against his wife for sending the strangers vainly into the fire for the child. The boy telling the story is appalled by the couple's incomprehensible reaction: "Surely there was some mystery, I said to myself, some questions that ought to be answered or asked." The mystery is accentuated by the imagery of the story, which suggests a descent into the nether world. Smoldering stumps, for instance, create an "infernal effect" over the whole scene, the woman looks like a "death's-head," and the two Good Samaritans resemble hooded pilgrims.

If the infernal experience is a new experience for the narrator, it is only commonplace to the older "pilgrims": "It was as if such a fire were an every-day occurrence in their lives and as if they lived always among such queer people as that afflicted poor-white farmer and his simple wife." The uncle and his friend refuse to accept the narrator's characterization of the place as "god-forsaken" or even as "ugly." "Every countryside has its own kind of beauty," the uncle says. "It's up to you to learn to see it, that's all." The lawyer friend adds: "And if you don't see it, it's just your loss. Because it's *there*." The only help they offer is the advice that "you would have to have seen that country thirty years ago to understand why it looks the way it does now."

Some things, then, Taylor seems to say, we are born accepting as natural and only with maturity come to recognize as mysterious, as "A Strange Story" points out. Other things we first take to be mysterious only to accept them as natural as age increases our experiences and, presumably, our wisdom, as "Two Pilgrims" indicates.

"Born to Represent Something"

"Miss Leonora When Last Seen," the title story of Taylor's 1963 volume, explores the mystery that can underlie any individual's life. The eccentric Miss Leonora Logan is "quite an old lady," a retired schoolteacher, and "the last of the Logan family in Thomasville, a family that for a hundred years and more did all it could to impede the growth and progress" of the town. Because the county court has just condemned her inherited property to provide a site for the county's new consolidated high school, Miss Leonora has taken off in her 1942 Dodge convertible for parts unknown. Though she has taken such trips before, the indications are that this time she may not be coming back. Her cryptic postcards back to her old pupils suggest only that she is circling through the surrounding states, "orbiting her native state of Tennessee."

The narrator, who was the first of Miss Leonora's "favorites" among her old students, fills in the background about her life and personality, as much as this can be done: "Miss Leonora is an intellectual woman, and at the same time she is an extremely practical and simple kind of person. This makes it hard for any two people to agree on what she is really like. It is hard even for those of us who were her favorites when we went to school to her. For, in the end, we didn't really know her any better than anybody else did." The narrator still recalls his first blinding vision of Miss Leonora, when he at the age of five feverishly watched Miss Leonora, all dressed in white and with a "burning beauty" in her countenance, step ashore from a picnicker's rowboat as if she had "risen out of the water itself." That vision pierced his soul, he says, and awoke him to a beauty he had not dreamed of.

Other pictures supplement this early vision of her—sharp images of Miss Leonora standing out in a crowd at a drowning and at a fire at the old Thomasville Female Institute, of Miss Leonora entertaining her favorite students with coffee and cookies and conversation about "*Silas Marner* or Tom Paine or Cicero," of Miss Leonora off on one of her trips in either "a lot of outmoded finery" or in her dungarees and big poke bonnet. Always Miss Leonora is the individualist who has her own ideas about what is good for Thomasville and for her favorites. For Thomasville, she agrees with her Logan ancestors that everything should be kept out that might possibly spoil the sweet dream of the town—things like a railroad, a county courthouse, a snuff factory or a cotton mill, a veterans' hospital, or a Civilian Conservation Corps camp. For those few students she has favored over the years, she urges a college education and entry into one of the professions in order "to populate the town with the sort of people she thought it ought to have." Her "mission" is the instruction of the town in her own values. "Looking back on those high-school days," the narrator says, "I know that all along she was watching me and others like me for some kind of sign from us—any sign—that would make us seem worthy of knowing what we wanted to know about her."

None of Miss Leonora's favorites ever really gives her this sign. Only one goes to college, and he comes back a pharmacist, not a physician; the narrator himself is nothing more than a hotel operator. And it is only in retrospect that these ex-students even understand what it was they wanted to know: "that the old lady had suffered for being just what she was—for being born . . . to represent something that had never taken root in Thomasville and that would surely die with her." The pathos of her chosen role becomes clear only after the narrator breaks the news to her about the county's dispossessing her of her property and after she takes off on her last journey.

The terrible shock of the story is that Miss Leonora "when last seen" is no longer the eccentric individualist she has always been before. Instead of setting off in her fox-fur piece, diamond earrings, velvet hat, and lace choker, or in her other traveling costume of home-knit cardigan and dungarees, Miss Leonora (like Aunt Munsie in the earlier "What You Hear from 'Em?" and like the grandfather in the later "In the Miro District") has transformed herself into an ordinary person. The narrator notes that all she now needs is "a pair of pixie glasses with rhinestone rims" and "a half dozen bracelets on her wrist" to pass for a Memphis matron "looking for antiques and country hams" and exclaiming with delight over finding "a southern town that is truly unchanged."

But Miss Leonora has changed in more than appearance. She begins to say things that are "nothing like the things the real Miss Leonora used to say," but that are things "anybody might have said." One of these things is her admission that she was "unrealistic" in trying to be to the Thomasville children what she thought they "needed to have somebody be" instead of "what they want one to be." To the narrator, then, it is a little sad to think of Miss Leonora alone in her old Dodge after her "change of heart," "wishing that either she had played the role of the spinster great lady the way it is usually played or that she had married some dirt farmer and spent her life working alongside him in the fields." With her role abandoned, there is no use even looking for her. "She will look too much like a thousand others," the narrator says, "and no doubt will be driving on the highway the way everybody else does, letting other people pass her, dimming her lights for everyone."

Maybe the narrator is right when he says that "times do change, and the interests of one individual cannot be allowed to hinder the progress of a whole community." And maybe he is also right when he argues that Miss Leonora's periodic auto trips have been "escapes into a reality that is scattered in bits and pieces along the highways and back roads of the country she travels." But Peter Taylor, who views "Miss Leonora When Last Seen" as almost a "complete allegory" and one of his best and most carefully constructed stories,[2] seems to suggest between the lines that the community pays a high price for progress when it suffers the loss of the last remaining "witness" to its "traditions and institutions" that have been corrupted or lost. Mystery though it may be, that witness's life has a meaning that nothing can ever duplicate.

"Beyond All the Good Sense and Reasonableness"

Still more engrossing than the mystery of another's life and personality is the mystery of self, a mystery elucidated in "At the Drugstore," perhaps the most resonantly symbolic story in *Miss Leonora*.

The hero of "At the Drugstore" is Matt Donelson, a man of thirty-five "back home on a visit," who drops in one early morning at the neighborhood drugstore where, as a teenager, he used to wait with his schoolmates for the special streetcar to the Country Day School. Ostensibly Matt has returned to this haunt of his youth only to buy a bottle of shaving lotion, but unconsciously he is searching for an image of himself in the surroundings of his earlier, formative years. Rising as he did at daybreak, while his parents, his wife, and his two boys are still sleeping, and seeing again the familiar cityscape, he feels his presence is "unreal," dreamlike, somehow dismaying. He recalls his arrival at the Union Depot the night before, where the remodeling of the depot lobby caused him momentarily to think himself in the wrong city.

The drugstore is also changed—except for the familiar pattern of the tile floor and the presence of the same old druggist of years past. In the artificial indigo tint of the fluorescent lights and in the early morning silence, Matt feels the drugstore has the "timeless quality" of a bank vault or a "small, out-of-the-way museum where the curator doesn't really expect or welcome visitors." When Matt sees not only the familiar face of Mr. Conway, the druggist, but, in the mirror behind Mr. Conway, "another familiar face (oh, *too familiar*)," he self-defensively puts on "the most impersonal, hard, out-of-town voice" he can muster. Later, the face in the mirror seems not the guilty schoolboy face from the past it had seemed at first, but the face of an intruder, a "third, unfamiliar person on the scene, a person who, so to speak, ought still to have been asleep beside his wife back there in the family's guest room." This face, moreover, has expressed in its look, without his consciously putting it there, the same "impersonal, hard, out-of-town" quality he had consciously put in his voice.

Memories sweep over Matt Donelson as he finds excuses to linger in the store. He recalls, particularly, the harassments (mischievous and sometimes even obscene) that the Country Day boys had once piled on Mr. Conway, but that Matt himself had never taken part in. So well does he remember the old image of Mr. Conway as an authority figure, that he finds himself at one point "momentarily insane" with repressed rage and ready to assault "the old Scrooge, the old bastard." The scrap between the two is avoided, but Matt knows that he will never be able to explain to anyone how near he came to unprecedented violence. "How unlike him it would have been, what an anomaly, how incongruous with everything else in a life that was going so well."

As he returns home for breakfast with his parents, his wife, and his children, he alternates between feelings of elation and feelings of despair and "of some other emotion less easily or less willingly identified . . . like regret for lost opportunities." The barrier he still feels between himself and his family can only be explained by a "kind of nonsense":

> It seemed to him now that he had gone to that drugstore on purpose this morning, that he had planned the whole adventure before he ever left New York. It had been intended to satisfy some passing and unnamed need of his, but the adventure had cut too deep into his memory and into what was far more than mere memory. Inadvertently he had penetrated beyond all the good sense and reasonableness that made life seem worthwhile—or even tolerable. And through the breach, beyond, behind or

beneath all this, he was now confronted by a thing that had a face and a will of its own. It was there threatening not only him and his father but the others too. Its threat was always present really, in him and in every man. It was in women too, no doubt, but they were so constituted that they never lost sight of it, were always on their guard, were dealing with it every moment of their lives. (*ML,* 78; *CS,* 137)

This nameless "Thing" he finally recognizes, catching a glimpse of his own reflection in the glass of a dark still-life painting (dead fish and dead, dull pheasants) above the family sideboard; the reflection appears to him "as the very face of that Thing he had uncovered," a "monstrous obtrusion on the relatively bright scene that was reflected all around it—the innocent scene at the breakfast table behind Matt." Observing the happy chattering family, he thinks: "How dearly he loved them all! And how bitterly the Thing showing its face in the glass hated them!"

Though Matt himself soon laughingly dismisses the "nonsense" about the "boogy man in the glass," the reader cannot so easily forget it. And when Matt, reconciled and united in a new understanding with his father and his family, dramatically peels his breakfast orange without a single break on the "thin inner pellicle" and lifts up the fruit "unscathed and whole" for all to see, the reader senses he has watched the excision and contemplation of something far more significant than an ordinary orange. He has, symbolically at least, seen the soul of a moral man.

"Delving into a Trunk"

Taylor's second retrospective collection, *Collected Stories,* in addition to sixteen previously collected stories, contains five new tales that are on the whole a bit less inventive than the new stories in *Miss Leonora.*

The theme of betrayal, present to some degree in works throughout Taylor's career, comes to the fore in two new stories, "Dean of Men" and "First Heat," that open the volume. "Dean of Men," another leisurely three-generation memoir story, represents a college administrator telling his student son how the boy's great-grandfather, grandfather, and father had all suffered different kinds of betrayal and how each had had to seek afterwards a way to "somehow go on living among men"; "it is a strange world," he says, "in which an old man must tell a young man this." Although Taylor's own father and grandfather suffered similar betrayals, Taylor has said the story is "not one of my favorites" because "the context is not as interesting." The father needs to tell the story to justify his life to his son, Taylor says, but "the son will not profit from it; his father has sold out to become Dean."[3]

"First Heat," a short straightforward dramatic story, treats betrayal from the point of view of the betrayer: a state senator must face his conscience in the person of his wife after he has withdrawn his promised support from a colleague on a crucial vote. While neither "First Heat" or "Dean of Men" breaks much new ground in matter of form, both stories show the usual Taylor craftsmanship in their development.

Two other new works in *Collected Stories* are mildly impressive echoes of themes from the *The Widows of Thornton*. "Mrs. Billingsby's Wine," a story about a young Memphis housewife calling on a grande dame from her old hometown, is rather artificially told in the historical present in the manner of the very early story "Allegiance." The young woman, Shirley Barnes, expects to be snubbed by the dowager, Mrs. Billingsby, but hopes eventually to win her patronage for her own social climbing. Surprisingly, Mrs. Billingsby is gracious and friendly and she happily reminisces with Shirley over their hometown of Blackwell, Tennessee. Listening to her, however, Shirley realizes that, though they were once next-door neighbors, their differences in social status, age, and attitude toward urban progress leave them no common ground; even their memories of Blackwell seem to be of two separate towns.

"The Elect," Taylor's first story since "The Dark Walk" to be published in one of the slick women's magazines, describes the emotions of the domestically inclined wife of a gubernatorial candidate the day after her husband wins the election. Her relief that the campaign ordeal of living like "show people" is over turns to an unnamed anxiety as she waits her husband's thanks for her campaign assistance. The anxiety turns first to tears and then to stoic resignation when she finally realizes her husband wants her to continue the public role she hates. Never again will she have the old domestic pleasures of paying her own household bills, of hemming her own skirts, or knowing the arrangement of her own kitchen. Like the biblical Ruth, whom she had once cited on a campaign platform, she must follow her husband whither he goes and his show people must now be her people, for she is one of the "elect" who are chosen from the many called to take on uncongenial duties in an ever-changing world.

The most complex in both form and content of the new pieces in *Collected Stories* is "There," a story that had been previously honored by inclusion in both the O. Henry *Prize Stories 1965* and *The Best American Short Stories of 1965*. In "There" a first-person narrator meets on board a ship a stranger from his hometown (a nameless "inland city") and finds himself listening to a long monologue full of subjective reminiscing. The two are united by their common point of origin and their common estrangement from that origin. But the middle-aged narrator also feels that the elderly Mr. Charles Varnell is "the kind of shipboard acquaintance you make who never seems real afterward" and that the thirty or forty years that separate them in age make them "strangers to one another" as "no distance across the surface of the earth nowadays, and no difference in nationality," could possibly do. The old man, though reticent about himself, is "voluble enough on other subjects—particularly on the subject of *other* people." And it is memories of the people back *there* in the hometown that touch him off.

In that city were the Busbys, the old man recalls, who never washed. And the Jenkinses who all got extremely fat. "It used to seem to me that every family there had some awful deficiency—I might almost say affliction—that marked them as a family," Mr. Varnell says. "The astonishing thing to me was always that the Busbys, like the Jenkinses and other families with equally marked peculiarities, remained in the very cream of society *there.* Nobody ever minded them as they were, and so why need they change themselves?" The one family he had found "interesting and admirable" was the Morris family, each member of which was distinguished for individuality and apparent lack of family traits. When he was a young man studying for a diplomatic career, Mr. Varnell fell in love with pretty Laura Nell, the practical joker of the Morris family, who chided Varnell for his inability to forgive people their faults. Laura Nell made a bargain then with Varnell: if he could guess the secret terrible trait the individualistic Morrises all had in common, then she would forgive him everything. Varnell eventually found out from Laura Nell's mother that the girl was alluding to a grim little joke of her grandfather's: "He used to say that the Morrises were all alike in at least one respect: they all had to die some time or other." Laura Nell's last practical joke is to prove the grandfather right—by contracting an inexplicable fatal disease and dying.

Varnell is, then, a kind of cross between Melville's Taji in *Mardi* and Hawthorne's Aylmer in "The Birthmark." Like Taji, he is contemptuous of the flawed human beings about him and searches for a phantom ideal in the person of an elusive maiden. Like Aylmer, he discovers mortality, the family flaw or birthmark that all humans, even those closest to the ideal, must share. But Varnell's story is not the transparent allegory that the comparison might suggest. Between Hawthorne-Melville and Peter Taylor intervened Henry James, and the Jamesian method makes all the difference. Taylor has not presented Varnell's story directly but has placed it in a narrative frame of the sort James used in the *The Turn of the Screw.* Varnell himself is a half century removed from his own experience; he is, we are told, "like a man delving into a trunk he had packed away years ago and who did not know, himself, what he would come upon next." And the first narrator, who, as we have already seen, considers himself an inevitable stranger to Varnell, refracts the meaning as the story passes through his mediating consciousness. Every literal detail therefore undergoes at least three stages of ironic qualification: Varnell's mature sophistication enables him to recognize a certain foolishness in his early point of view; the first narrator's academic detachment permits him to detect blind spots even in Varnell's present vision; and, between the lines, Taylor's own auctorial presence suggests the limitations of the first narrator's insight.

Chapter Eight

Back to the Boards

An Inclination to Other Forms

"I doubt that I'll write many more short stories," Peter Taylor told Stephen Goodwin in 1973. "I feel that I've done what I want to do as a short story writer. For years I was so absorbed in stories that I didn't think I would ever try to do anything else, but when I start a story now, I know that I can write it. Once you've learned how to do something as well as you can, you just don't care about repeating it."[1]

Although more stories, including some of his best, would still come from his pen, Taylor from some point in the mid-sixties to the present has been continually butting against the constraints of the form in which he had established his distinguished reputation, trying in several different ways to break the genre barrier that had hitherto largely confined his talent. The novelette *A Woman of Means* and the two early plays *The Death of a Kinsman* and *Tennessee Day in St. Louis* had already indicated some inclination to try other forms, but they hardly presaged the near-abandonment in the seventies and eighties of his previous stock in trade. The work of Peter Taylor's mature career has been directed (sometimes alternately, sometimes simultaneously) toward drama, toward verse narrative, and toward the novel.

Of these, playwriting apparently had the earliest and most compelling attraction, because Taylor has always felt "that the short story is a dramatic form and that it's much more natural for a short story writer to write plays than it is for him to write novels," as he thinks the careers of Chekhov, Pirandello, and the Irish playwrights prove.[2] The seriousness of Taylor's commitment to working in the dramatic medium is indicated by his traveling to London in 1961 to spend a year (under a Ford Foundation grant) studying practical theater techniques at the Royal Court repertory theater.

The stage histories of *The Death of a Kinsman* and *Tennessee Day in St. Louis* could hardly have encouraged him. Although Taylor experienced amateur and college productions ranging from the "very satisfying" to the "excruciatingly painful," he didn't get to see a television production of *Tennessee Day* which was done by a St. Louis station and he had his hopes for Broadway or other New York productions continually dashed.[3] Further, most critical commentary on the two early plays, while generally responsive to their themes, regarded them as reasonably stimulating considered as closet drama but only half-realized considered as practical theater. Apparently undaunted, Taylor confessed in an interview: "I would like to spend most of my time writing plays. I'd like to have the plays produced, but I'm also terribly interested in having them read." He tries to write, he says, for those rare people who love to read plays; consequently, he cares "very much" about the language, trying "to make each line work, make it interesting and revealing, just as . . . in a story." "There are themes and experiences," he has further observed, "that fiction simply can't handle convincingly."[4]

The four-year period between 1970 and 1973 saw the longest pause in Taylor's story-publishing career—not a single new story came before the public. During that period, however, he published eight one-act plays, signaling that his productivity was simply being channelled into a new genre. Although at least four other major plays have been reported in progress from time to time, these eight short plays of the 1970–73 period and one slightly earlier full-length drama, *A Stand in the Mountains* (originally published in 1968 in *Kenyon Review* but not brought out in hardcover until 1985),[5] constitute the only results of his later playwriting phase that have so far been exposed to reader scrutiny. Of these, Taylor clearly regards *A Stand in the Mountains* as his chef d'oeuvre, agreeing with an interviewer that it may be "the best thing" he's ever written.[6]

"A Class unto Themselves"

Originally called *The Girl from Forkèd Deer, A Stand in the Mountains* had been gestating for years. It was much revised and expanded just days before its initial magazine publication, and it underwent additional revision sometime prior to its book publication seventeen years later. Taylor has described it as the first of a planned trilogy of plays all with the same setting: the resort area of Sewanee and Monteagle, Tennessee, redesignated fictionally as "Owl Mountain." The play's final title, suggested by Donald Davidson's poem "Lee in the Mountains," alludes to the cherished Southern idea that Robert E. Lee, had he been allowed to make a last stand in the mountains, "might have held out indefinitely."[7]

For Owl Mountain, his slightly disguised Cumberland Mountain resort, Taylor has invented a detailed Faulknerian history, printed in a long elegiac preface to the play. The main characters are Taylor's usual wealthy urban Southerners, known on Owl Mountain as "the summer people." But there are also two characters representing a type not found in other Taylor works: the primitive, racially mixed mountaineers who have eked out impoverished existences on the depleted plateaus for some two hundred years.

As in *Tennessee Day,* this play also opens on a festive occasion—the Fourth of July, the opening of the resort season. Louisa Weaver, the socially prominent widow of a rich Louisville lawyer, has returned to her Owl Mountain cottage with her retinue in tow. The entourage includes her aging but devoted brother-in-law, Will Weaver; a young country cousin, Mina, whom she hopes to introduce to Louisville society in the fall; and, much to her own surprise, her twenty-eight-year-old son Zach, a poet, who has just turned up at home after a rebellious sojourn in Italy. Already at Owl Mountain is Louisa's elder son, Harry, who "in defiance of Louisa's wishes and her strong will" had at an early age married a mountain girl and embraced the primitive life of the mountaineers. These characters are joined later by Georgia Morris, a former protégée of Louisa's, who ran away in the middle of her debutante season and who is now the wife of an Italian nobleman and the mistress of Louisa's son Zach.

In the seven scenes that constitute the play, complications come quickly. Zach falls in love with Mina, who is already in love with Harry, and Harry falls in love with Georgia. By the end of the third scene Harry has shot and wounded his mountain wife, Lucille; by the end of the fifth scene he has fatally broken her neck; by the end of the sixth scene he has shot and killed his wife's grandmother, his two sons, and himself. Though it is all offstage, there is more intrigue and violent action in this play than in any other of Taylor's works.

Unfortunately, the violent climax seems only tenuously related to the most interesting conflicts of the play, which all involve the ambivalent relationships of the other characters to Louisa, who is simultaneously as charming and as exasperating as Madame Ranevksy of *The Cherry Orchard.* Harry and Zach are both unhappy sons still trying to "take revenge" on the mother who would have made "male debutantes" out of them, and Uncle Will admits that his long, silent ardor for Louisa has been like that of an anxious child for its mother. All three men react to the other women (including Louisa's offstage stepdaughters whom Zach refers to as "Goneril and Regan") as if they were only mirrored aspects of Louisa. "What is it they have all done to us?" Zach asks, alluding to "the female conspiracy." "Let's go into the ladies now," Harry says a little later; "let's face the real enemy." By turning respectively to history, to poetry, and to atavistic flight, Will, Zach, and Harry attempt to escape woman's supposed ineluctable purpose of ruling men.

At the heart of this conflict are some of the same concerns about women's roles that figured in *Tennessee Day.* Louisa has come from one kind of milieu, the Southern country town, and she has found herself without a clear role in her new milieu, the affluent urban high society. Her preoccupation with the American debutante "institution" is her effort to define her own status. The country cousins she perennially presents to society are, in Mina's words, "her link between Forkèd Deer and Louisville, between the world she came out of and the world she lives in." Louisa has had to make "the best out of all the possibilities her life offered," and her efforts have sometimes seemed misguided. "To most people she seems the epitome of femaleness," Harry says. "Yet underneath she operates like a man." Later Harry explains further: "She doesn't know that American women are becoming men and men are becoming women. She doesn't know there is no such thing as a woman's world and a man's world nowadays. She doesn't know what a blur the whole world has become."

Louisa, Georgia, and Mina are all attempting to accommodate themselves to this blurry world, just as Auntie Bet, Lucy, and Nancy were in *Tennessee Day;* and there are striking parallels between the two sets of characters—both male and female—in the two plays. It is only when Lucille, the exemplar of primitive woman, also becomes demanding and determined to seek her own "advantages" in the manner of Louisa or Mina, that Harry goes on his berserk rampage. This rampage is Harry's form of what Georgia calls her own new "religion": "You've got to be willing to cut loose, no matter what you get yourself into—cut loose from your own innocent, little children even, if your life requires it." For men, the alternative to cutting loose, as the drunken "oinking" of the three men at the end of the sixth scene suggests, is to become swine in some Circe's pen.

All these personal stories in *A Stand in the Mountains* are so closely linked to the historical and sociological peculiarities of the setting that their drama plays almost like an allegorical tableau about the South's beleaguered and endangered cultural inheritance. Taylor has acknowledged that *A Stand in the Mountains* depicts "a different world from the world I began writing about where families did exist as little groups, and if they went out of the South, they took the South with them." Since that habit of Southerners carrying the South with them is no longer so prevalent, Taylor says his present concern "is for what sort of adjustments we are making to this, how we shall live without it."[8]

In his preface's detailed analysis of his characters' social background Taylor calls his summer people "the sons and daughters of the old regime who have had too much energy, too much vitality to be willing to accept shabby gentility as a way of life"; they are, he says, "those whose forebears left the land a generation or so ago, and with their good names and their connections and their natural endowments went to the new Southern cities and towns to make a place for themselves." Though they appeared to abandon "the old order of life and the old Cause," in their hearts and minds "they did not really do so"; their talk, therefore, is "always apt to be of the old days, the old ways, the old places." They thus remain to the present "a class unto themselves," holing up for "a last stand together" in the decaying mountain resort that reminds them somehow of "all the old country towns they had left behind." Taylor further insists in the preface that all the "gentry" characters in the play "suffer in some degree from the emptiness of the old roles they are playing, and their suffering is increased whenever they try to make some sense out of their roles." In Taylor's stories with similar themes, we have little difficulty accepting such generalizations about characters, because our experience of the characters is mediated through a narrative consciousness—a consciousness similar to that of the auctorial voice in this play's preface. In the play itself, however, we must base our inferences only on what the characters can be seen doing or heard saying, and Taylor seems not to have given us external correlatives sufficient to convey all those interior attitudes that are the real subject described in the preface.

A Stand in the Mountains has no paucity of dramatic ideas or provocative themes. It toys with such intriguing topics as the failure of the cities as centers of power and culture, the erosion of place distinctions so that "all places are alike," the quasi-religious aspects of the debutante system, the loss of "the Old America," and the lure of the native clay (literally for Harry and Georgia, who are ceramicists, and figuratively for everyone else). But too many of the characters and subplot complications seem superfluous, dragged awkwardly in to illustrate tangential motifs that Taylor could not bring himself to discard, however distracting they might be to dramatic cohesiveness.

"Certain Encumbrances"

Taylor followed *A Stand in the Mountains* with a series of one-act ghost plays which he collected in the 1973 volume *Presences: Seven Dramatic Pieces.*[9] The common element in the seven plays is the externalized presence of ghosts or fantasies, which Taylor believes are part of our common experience and which can tell us things about ourselves we "could not otherwise know."[10] But the choice of the ghost motif, he acknowledges, dictated the choice of the dramatic medium:

> Before putting pen to paper, I gave considerable thought to how I might best present such experience and have it believed and felt. I came to the conclusion that ghosts as well as the fantasies that we invent about living people require too much artifice when presented in fiction . . . [.] Whereas in a play, the ghost simply walks upon the stage. We do not question his presence. He is as real to us as any natural character in a play; he seems as real to us in the audience as he does to the other character or characters who, out of their urgent need or unbearable fear, have created his presence through their imagination.[11]

Each of these plays, then, objectifies as some kind of ghostly presence some image, influence, or emotional baggage that haunts the lives of one or more characters. These materialized ghostly presences derive their identities from the memories, fantasies, and projected roles of the flesh-and-blood people to whom they appear. "I'm coming," the old lady Maisie (in *A Voice through the Door*) responds to a knock while hurriedly hiding the ghosts in her room, ". . . But I have certain encumbrances." And that essentially is what the ghosts are: encumbrances the characters must struggle under or against. Taylor has often attempted to represent similar encumbrances symbolically in his fiction, as in "The Dark Walk," where the widowed Sylvia Harrison finally realizes that the furniture she had carried with her from city to city throughout all the moves of her married life had been the sign of her bondage to "all that was old and useless and inherited." The characters in *Presences* are no freer than Sylvia, though their psychological and spiritual encumbrances are here represented as spectral visions rather than as a van full of furniture.

The first play, *Two Images,* introduces us to a thirty-five-year-old much-divorced woman, Meg, and her younger brother, Nicky, as they summon up opposing apparitions of their deceased father. To Nicky, who remembers his father as a philanderer, hypocrite, and bully, the ghost of a silent, overweight, disheveled, middle-aged man appears; the ghost has to take Nicky's lectures, orders, and verbal abuse just the way Nicky once had to submit to his father. To Meg, who has idealized her father as a man who dedicated his life to his children, a slender, straight, correctly dressed, and highly dignified ghost approaches her seductively; at curtain close, she succumbs to his lover's embrace. Nicky's ghost had come to him many times before, but Meg's ghost could materialize only after Nicky's reminiscences of his father's sexual promiscuity made Meg let herself see him. The ghost specifically tells Meg, "I am just what I always was, am I not, Meg?" In short, the point the play makes somewhat too explicitly is that Meg's erotic attachment to her father had always been a presence (throughout all four loveless marriages) but could not be faced for what it was until her idealized image of the father was transformed and released by Nicky's iconoclastic countervision.

The second play, *A Father and a Son,* also is built on the device of two images of a dead person, although in this instance the images are remarkably similar, albeit equally imperceptive. The single subject of the images is the daughter of old Nathan and the mother of young Jack; she regularly visits both her father and her son as a ghostly minister, attending to their emotional needs. But they—her father and her son—have no real understanding of her or of her unselfish passion for her husband, whom both Nathan and Jack jealously resented and despised. "Poor darlings," she says of them to her husband who has lately joined her in death. "If only they could understand what it is to love someone." The father and the son know she comes to them because they need her; they cannot seem to realize, however, that her ne'er-do-well husband needed her even more and so her commitment to him was even more engrossing and enduring. "It's your *presence* that *is* everything," Nathan once tells his daughter's ghost, cherishing her memory when, if he had been more willing to share, he might have been enjoying her reality.

The ghost in the third play, *Missing Person,* is not a memory of another person but a character's projection of himself into "what might have been." On a lecture trip to his old hometown, Virgil Minor, a successful novelist, spends an evening with his old sweetheart, Flo Abbot, now a widowed mother of three children. As the evening wears on, they recall another side of Virgil that would have been content in the hometown the way Flo has been. As Virgil admits:

> There was another side to me once. When we are young we all have more sides than one . . . . It seems almost impossible that those other aspects of one's self besides the one you finally concentrate upon, don't go on developing somewhere. I've kept thinking all day today about that other side of me you refer to. Was he around somewhere? Would I see him? (*PSDP,* 66)

Later, as the lights blink on and off in a storm, the "missing person" appears and Virgil sees himself as he might have been as Flo's bourgeois husband. This alter ego confesses, "I've had to do things *you* couldn't have brought yourself to do," but he is unable to tell Virgil whether these things were "worth it." Flo perceives that Virgil has seen this "missing person" and confides that he is "always here" in her house, where he, not the real-life Virgil, has been the object of her love and yearning. Flo and Virgil then part, lamenting the terrible "narrowness" that has doomed them to be only one aspect of themselves.[12]

Whistler, the fourth play, also involves projections of the "might have been." In this instance Emma and Harry Patterson recall their fears for their son Tom, who is now "missing in action" in an unspecified war, presumably Vietnam. Harry had feared that Tom would be a long-haired, hippie conscientious objector; Emma had feared he would become an animal-like killer; both had failed to realize his life and death were not theirs to determine. Now Tom's ghost appears separately to each as the actualization of their worst fears. Each parent, however, welcomes the son just as he is—glad of his presence and oblivious to the once-dreaded role he now enacts. Tom's request to each before he disappears is that the other parent be told he is alive. But the play ends with the two grieving parents acknowledging together the death they can no longer deny.

The projection of fears is carried still further in the fifth play, entitled *Arson.* Rob, a student, returns to his mother's apartment with a young black radical, Leo, with whom he has been involved in the burning of a college building in a campus protest. The mother, Liz, implants in Rob's mind the idea that Leo is homosexually attached to him; Leo in turn suggests that Liz is incestuously possessive. Rob then fantasizes each of them approaching him in their hitherto unperceived roles. It seems to him a nightmare he is having, but a nightmare he must "finish out" by stripping off his clothes and building a ritual holocaust in the center of the apartment. Leo and Liz reappear in their ordinary guises, and Rob declares:

> It was only a dream—or a wish I had. It was not your real selves I saw. It was my own. It is myself, isn't it, I have exposed, revealed, disrobed, unmasked tonight. You two are only—always—what I wish for you to seem. And now I have wished you back the way you were. It's no good the other way. So we'll have another fire. (*PSDP,* 153–54)

As he lights the pyre at curtain close, he proclaims, "Fire also is only a wish—a dream of escape."

In some ways the most complex of all the plays in *Presences* is the next-to-last, *A Voice through the Door.* Here, Maisie, a septuagenarian maiden aunt, shares her suite in her niece's house with the ghosts of all her deceased relatives, who sit before her sewing, knitting, whispering, even chewing and spitting tobacco. All her life her family has "protected" her from various things, including an ill-advised romance in her youth. Now, her still-living family is protecting her from a visit by her grandnephew Bobby, who has shocked his parents by coming home from college with long hair and beard. Maisie hears a voice through the door and, despite veiled insinuations by her spectral companions, lets Bobby in. Maisie learns of Bobby's plans to live his life as he pleases and to go off on his own against the family's will; she asks him to express his feelings so she can share them vicariously. Bobby, in turn, confesses he returned home only because of Maisie, because he needed to see once more how she had done what he could never do: "always managing to go along with them," the domineering family. Eventually, the spirits of the kinfolk about her force Maisie to recognize that Bobby is another ghost, the spirit of her long-ago lover projected into the image of her grandnephew. Meantime, the real Bobby has succumbed to family pressure, shaved his offending beard, and promised to return to college. Maisie then forgets once more her long-lost lover, and the spirits of her kin promise to be with her to the end.

The seventh and final play in the collection, *The Sweethearts,* makes the theater audience a kind of ghostly presence, judging the propriety and decorum of the characters. At center stage, as it were, are Janet and Louis, a middle-aged couple who still enact the roles of sweethearts. "We are entitled to a life of our own, to being our*selves*—not always somebody's child or somebody's parent," Janet says defensively when they agree they were right to put Janet's senile mother in a "Home." Grandmom, a feisty old lady who appears to owe not a little to Edward Albee's Grandma in *The American Dream,* doesn't want to return to the Home, however, and she recognizes the "married sweethearts" as a dangerous enemy to everybody in the family, since "sweethearts *have* to be alone." Carol, the daughter of Janet and Louis, realizes the same thing when she tells her parents that she and her husband are planning an abortion and her parents turn away from her problem and back to their self-absorption as lovers. In near hysteria, Carol cries: "What a way of shutting out the world! What a way of forgetting about the life . . . of the child you don't ever have!" As both Grandma and Carol have made clear in earlier comments, the role of sweethearts is enacted before other people, represented by the theater audience, who "manage to carry on" through other types of "play-pretend."

Presences and Absences as Well

Just as the ghosts and spirits in *Presences* are concepts or fantasies that make themselves immanent in the lives of the characters, so there are typical themes and techniques of Peter Taylor that hover as literary "presences" throughout the sequence of plays. And just as the characters in the plays often have clarifying visions of their own ghosts, so readers of these plays can clearly see devices here that might be obscured from view in Taylor's other works. The plays force the revelation, for instance, of how often Taylor's characters represent abstractions manipulated in mathematical arrangements like factors in a formula. Frank Moore Colby once made fun of Henry James for the intellectual phantoms he passed off as characters and the demonstrations of theorems he passed off as plot; good Jamesian that he is, Peter Taylor may have more wraiths and bogies in his work than the labeled ghosts in these plays, for his story characters, too, are often arranged as opposing sets of values, operating as spectral encumbrances on each other. In particular, in Taylor's stories about Southern families (the majority of his stories) the assorted uncles and aunts and cousins and grandparents and in-laws and servants function as controlling presences that limit freedom and individuality of the group as a whole.

These little ghost plays are filled with contemporary motifs we do not at all associate with Taylor's usual terrain: incest, homosexuality, abortion, radicalism, student protest, war, arson, to name a few. But despite these atypical topics, what these same plays demonstrate more than anything else is how consistent and enduring Taylor's themes are regardless of genre, setting, or ostensible subject. In *Presences,* as in so many of his stories, inherited sex roles, the generation gap, and societal expectations again trap individuals into various kinds of compromises between sheer rebellion and abject capitulation. Every single play in *Presences* deals with families as manipulative, dominating forces with at least the potential to stifle individuality as the price for "protection" from a variety of sometimes unnamed external forces. *A Father and a Son,* for instance, depicts the living relatives speaking of the freedom their mutual kinswoman has gained in death; yet her servile attendance on them as a ghost suggests there is no freedom from the bondage of family love even after death. *A Voice through the Door* carries that theme to its logical development in the other direction, as it represents the living still in thrall to deceased kin who remain ever present. "But one thing I'm sure of," old Maisie says in this play, "the living cannot protect us from our dead, just as the dead cannot protect us from our living."

It is Maisie also who gives one of the most explicit revelations yet of the love-hate paradox that inextricably binds Taylor's families together. "It's tempting to follow certain inclinations one has, to be self-indulgent, but the love of one's family is like a different kind of yearning, hunger—one that must be satisfied as well as any other," Maisie says. "One can't entirely live without it if ever one has tasted family life, family love. And one should not try." Maisie then indulges in an explanation that the materialized presences of her deceased relatives drive home: "The family body is as real, as organic as the individual body. The fact that its various members can walk away, if they will, doesn't necessarily mean it is not as real and organic as a person. . . . The family must live, too, and sometimes one of its members must yield." From the spirit of her long-ago lover, Maisie finally learns how sometimes individuals can attain some freedom from family: "You don't do it against their love, or against their will. And you do not love them less. What you do, what you have to do, is make them not exist so much. You make yourself exist more. You must make yourself exist in someone else or something else you are going toward." This idea is almost precisely the revelation Taylor gave to Sylvia Harrison in "The Dark Walk" nearly twenty years before: "She knew, at least, that in the future she would regard the people she loved very differently from the way she had in the past. And it wasn't that she would love them less; it was that she would in some sense or other learn to love herself more."

Presences, then, recapitulates some of the pervading strengths of Peter Taylor's literary art. Yet probably few readers would find these plays as aesthetically satisfying as the best of Taylor's stories. There are felt "absences" as well as "presences" in these plays, and these absences are those fictional devices that served Taylor so well in his short stories but are here ruled out by the nature of the dramatic medium. We miss here such things as the unifying perspective of a central consciousness (either narrator or character), the digressive-progressive narrative technique, and above all the plethora of realistic and homely detail, the ambience of place, the tints and tones and moods that make up cultural context and provide the richness and texture of Taylor's stories. Perhaps because of the condensation inherent in the one-act format, we learn little about the likes, dislikes, tastes, attitudes, education, religion, hobbies, interests, ambitions, or frustrations of the characters—except for those few that bear upon the immediate dramatic conflict. The first three plays are set nominally in St. Louis, but without any of the delineation of place found in *A Woman of Means* or even in the play *Tennessee Day in St. Louis;* with the exception of *A Voice through the Door,* which has the most realistic detail, most of the plays could be set anywhere, with only some slight exaggeration in some characters' manners to suggest the South a little more than other regions.

Taylor is too conscious an artist not to know he was sacrificing something when he chose to write one-act plays about materialized abstractions. He clearly was aiming at a new and different type of effect—an effect with its own special measure of success.

A Sort of a Something

The final work of Peter Taylor's 1970s playwriting phase is *The Early Guest,* a most curious hybrid, subtitled in its first publication in *Shenandoah* as "a sort of a story, a sort of a play, a sort of a dream."[13] Its genesis, Taylor has said, was as a long novel he wrote in the 1960s, a novel he never published and eventually tore up because "the poetry of it didn't work, the poetry of character and context." The novel was intended to deal with the theme of an artist's complex relationship to his native cultural environment:

> It was about a young man in a city like Memphis, an artist, a painter, a writer, who goes away to New York. It's about his love affair with an older woman. Then years later he comes back. It's about his growing up and his discovery of the world outside, and his failures as an artist, really. But it never satisfied me—his relation to his background, and then his discovery of what he was to do with his life and how it related to the world he'd come out of.[14]

The Early Guest, Taylor says, is "a sort of synopsis" of the novel in play form, written "just to get it out of my system."[15]

What was originally a novel of some magnitude is reduced in *The Early Guest* to a scant twenty pages of dialogue between the older woman (Sue Hayes) and the writer/artist, her former lover (Frank Lacy), labeled simple as SHE and HE in the script. But despite its derivation from the presumably rich social detail of a novel, the play is stylized (almost minimalist) theater, not far removed in tone, theme, or technique from the plays in *Presences.* Its nonrepresentational quasi-expressionist format is signaled immediately by the appearance of both characters in masks—hers depicting the grotesque face of a very old woman, his the face of a handsome young man, though she is actually sixty-five years old, he almost fifty.

The play begins with Sue (now the immensely rich and socially respectable Mrs. Susanna Hayes-Hoffman) waiting in her second-floor sitting room, listening to the slamming car door, the ringing doorbell, and the mounting footstep on the stair that signal the earlier-than-expected arrival of Frank (now the famed Manhattan avant-garde editor/publisher Francis Lacy), whom she has imperiously summoned back to his hometown (the Memphis-like fictional city of Paxton) to become her executor and the adviser to her proposed foundation for the training of young artists. In great detail (sometimes in speeches up to twelve hundred words in length!) they recall the wild love affair they had when he was nineteen and she was thirty-five, their scandalizing of the entire city, and her final sending him off to New York to escape his provincial constraints and to discover himself as poet and novelist. Figuratively first, and then literally, as they bare old hurts and resentments, they strip off each other's masks.

Sue is bitter that Frank failed to deliver on his promise as an artist—failed to take advantage of the chance she gave him (through his escape from the "hell hole" of Paxton) to "do something" with his life and talent. He, in turn, seethes that she in fact ruined his life both by dismissing him as her lover and by removing him from the roots that could have nourished his art. "Ever since," he says, "I have been cursed in my own mind with the image of myself as a very young man, never able to take my own experience quite seriously or to imagine myself thoroughly mature. What had I to write novels and poems about? In your stupidity, which you mistook for worldly wisdom, you destroyed me." Although Sue avers "It is not true—neither your picture or mine," she accepts Frank's departing lament that they have no choice but to replace their masks and wear them the rest of their lives. Left alone, Sue resumes the masked posture she held when the curtain first rose, listening once more to the automobile, the doorbell, the footsteps. "It is really he! It is time now," she says, indicating the early guest was only a phantom. Now, ready to resume the dialogue with what must this time be the real Frank, she repeats the speech with which she began the play, ending with the reiterated line: "The past must not stand in my way."

The Early Guest thus examines from quite a different perspective the question also explored in *Missing Person* from *Presences.* In *Missing Person* the novelist Virgil Minor questions whether he could ever have achieved his work as a novelist had he not left his hometown for New York; in *The Early Guest* Frank Lacy adamantly insists, "it was only by staying in Paxton that I might have become an artist." These two "ghost" plays together, the only works of Taylor's mature period to deal in a substantial way with the subject of an artist's life, provide a sort of double coda for themes initially broached in the 1955 story "1939."

Like Taylor's other plays, *The Early Guest* has had only limited theatrical exposure and in that limited exposure has drawn mixed response. Commenting on two performances at the University of Virginia, Taylor the determined playwright remains undaunted: "There is absolutely not a laugh in the whole play, it's dead serious, without any irony, and one performance was done for a big audience, and I though it was an excellent flop. But then it was presented again to a small high-brow audience of people just wild about the theater, and I thought it was a great success—and that was some consolation."[16]

Chapter Nine

In the Miro District and *The Old Forest*

"A Lot More in a Short Space"

If his numerous forays into playwriting in the seventies show Peter Taylor struggling against the genre barrier in one direction, his next two books—*In the Miro District* (1977) and *The Old Forest* (1985)—reveal him struggling against that barrier again but in a quite different direction.

In the Miro District, Taylor's first all-new story collection in eighteen years, provides the clue to the new direction: four of its eight stories are printed in what appears to be a kind of free and irregular unrhymed verse. But these four "stoems" or "broken-line prose" narratives, as Taylor calls them, are only the visible remnants of what was indeed a wide-ranging experiment.[1] For Taylor has acknowledged that all of the stories from the seventies and eighties collected in either *In the Miro District* or *The Old Forest,* regardless of how they appear on the printed page, were originally written in the broken-line free-verse format. In addition, he has published five other still-uncollected verse stories in periodicals.[2]

"I began writing them when I was trying to make things shorter," Taylor has said. "I am always trying for compression. It fascinates me that my stories get longer and longer when I'm always trying to make them shorter and shorter." He further explains:

> I began by wanting to get interest in every line, every sentence. I felt if a line is broken, if where the line ends means something, you get another emphasis. When a sentence just ends at that line, you get one kind of rhythm, one emphasis, but if it ends in the middle of the line, you get something else, the run-on lines, enjambment. . . . You have the two kinds of syntax, the line-endings and the run-on line, and the regular syntax of the language. You can be saying a lot more in a short space.[3]

Because compression and intensity of effect are so important to a story, Taylor believes that in a certain way a short story "is somewhere between a novel and a poem"; further, the best short stories, like those of Chekhov, "are really poems" and "can be talked about as poems in the same way," since "you see the structure, you see it all at once, as you can't in the novel."[4] Consequently, he feels that in his fiction "every phrase must have some intrinsic interest as well as relate to the larger interest of the story."[5] His goal, then, in writing virtually all his recent fiction (even, apparently, his novel *A Summons to Memphis*[6]) in verse or broken-line prose, is "to make the language count, to make every word, every sentence, count more."[7]

Such a goal inevitably creates a new standard by which his work now needs to be judged.

The Risk of the Hybrid Form

When Taylor's first verselike broken-line stories began to appear in print, they served as a forceful reminder that Taylor had not only established his reputation over the previous thirty years or so as a *prose* writer, but as a *prosaic* writer whose language characteristically had the rambling, unpretentious simplicity of friendly conversation. Memorable images emerged, perhaps, from scenes or vignettes, but seldom from individual lines or phrases; figures of speech were sparse, except for the banal colloquialisms that might dot a middle-class Everyman's everyday patter. Editors have gratuitously reedited and reprinted Thomas Wolfe's lyrical prose in verse form, but who would ever have been tempted to do the same for Peter Taylor?

Yet, appearing on the page (by the author's own design) as verse, Taylor's stories immediately demand a second look (or listen) in terms of both their linguistic intensity and their poetic sensibility. Robert Penn Warren, in a jacket blurb on the original edition of *In the Miro District,* praised the "radically new technique," while Keith Cushman fairly well summed up the negative view of the "formal eccentricity": "Taylor takes a great risk in attempting this hybrid form, and what he winds up with is at best distracting. The stories look too much like poetry to be taken as prose, but read too much like prose to be taken as poetry."[8]

Although some of Taylor's still-uncollected broken-line narratives have subjects conventionally associated with the poetic realm (e.g., "Peach Trees Gone Wild in the Lane," "Five Miles from Home"), none of the four verse stories in *In the Miro District* have topics that would ordinarily mandate poetic treatment. All four, in fact, cover fairly familiar Taylor territory and do not have content significantly different in kind from other stories in this and previous Taylor collections.[9] Yet each has at least some natural affinity with a recognized poetic form.

"The Instruction of a Mistress," the first verse narrative to be encountered in *In the Miro District,* has the most readily recognizable conventions. The story consists of three related dramatic monologues, emulating in a modern way the form made popular by Browning and Tennyson. Here, though, the monologues are imagined as written, not spoken; the first and third are from the journal of a distinguished poet, the second is a letter written by the poet's young mistress and protégée. The plot emerges as an ironic reworking of the Pygmalion-Galatea myth in the circles of contemporary literati. Like the mythological sculptor, the poet in this story creates the object of his affection, not out of stone this time, but out of an uncouth, ungainly, ill-read student. In the first monologue he brags of the transformations he has wrought in her: "I taught her more in five years / Than she might otherwise have learnt in twenty"; "Only let it be said: I was her college education"; "My friends did finally like her. / They saw her transformed before their eyes. / Partly, I suppose, they liked her just for that, / Out of a kind of appreciation for the miracle / And partly, I think, because they were happy to see / I could *still* inspire such love and such change / In a young girl."

In the second monologue—"an old letter found posthumously among her possessions"—we discover that the creature herself manipulated and controlled the creator. The young mistress in this letter to her lesbian lover alludes to the "daring," "underhanded," "wicked" scheme that brought her to the poet: a scheme to insinuate herself into his affection until she could identify the mysterious love who inspired his poems and could use this information for a book she and her woman lover hoped to write about "the germ of his creativity." But the mistress finds herself caught up in her new world and reluctant to leave it even for her chosen inamorata; she is strangely intent on making the poet love her as he had his earlier inspirational love. The final monologue, a journal entry by the poet after the girl's death in an automobile "accident," finds the poet comparing her death to that of the inspirational love of his youth—who, it turns out, was a boy in his class at an old-fashioned Latin school, who killed himself when his advances were rejected by the poet and who was then re-created in imagination by the poet in his poems. "We must create creatures whom we can love," the poet concludes, as he prepares to transform a new protégée he has already brought under his wing.

If "The Instruction of a Mistress" has Browningesque ironies throughout, the next verse-tale, "The Hand of Emmagene," has echoes of the English ballad tradition. Though the narrator is a civilized urban gentleman, the focal character is his wife's country cousin, Emmagene, a rural primitive with values and beliefs as ancient and mysterious as the backwoods from which she abruptly emerges. Emmagene's city cousins do not know quite what to make of her or what to do with her when she comes to stay at their house while attending secretarial school, but "from the very beginning" they have in mind that "she ought to know some boys / Her own age." Unfortunately, Emmagene is too plain and puritanical for the country club set and will have nothing to do with the shadowy swains from her hometown who migrate to the city and swarm covertly around her. Egged on by her hosts, Emmagene at last consents to consort with the country youths, but her conscience is clearly troubled.

> "This boy George doesn't really misbehave with you,
> Does he, Emmagene?" Nancy asked her. "Because if he does,
> Then you mustn't, after all, go out with him—
> With him or with the others."
> "You know I wouldn't let him do that, Cousin Nan," she said.
> "Not really. Not the real thing, Cousin Nan."
> "What do you mean?" Nancy asked in genuine bewilderment.
> The girl looked down at her hands, which were folded in her lap.
> "I mean, it's my hands he likes," she said.
> And she quickly put both her hands behind her, out of sight.
> "It's what they all like if they can't have it any other way."
> (*IMD*, 96)

When her city hosts cannot contain their horror at this revelation, Emmagene cuts off—literally—the hand that offended:

> What we saw in the kitchen was the blood everywhere.
> And the ax lying in the middle of the linoleum floor
> With the smeary trail of blood it left
> When she sent it flying.
> (*IMD*, 99)

The Gothic qualities of this denouement, highly unusual for Taylor, would be right at home in the ballad world of demon lovers, unforgivable sins, and cruel revenges.

"Her Need," the third story-poem, is a bit reminiscent of the poetic character portraits of such modern poets as E. A. Robinson ("Aunt Imogen," for instance) or Robert Frost ("Home Burial," "Paul's Wife," etc.). Bit by bit, the curtain is pulled back to reveal the inner conflicts, the drives, and (as the title underlines) the needs of a contemporary career woman, who is trying to function as single parent of a teenage son and as a rising executive of a bank. Only now, in mid-life, have her demonstrated competence and efficiency brought her the recognition that she should have had twenty years before. Belatedly, her boss tells her, "We think you're a whizz!" It chafes her that nobody had ever given her a clue in her girlhood "That she was a whizz / Or might become a whizz"; it chafes her even more that her adolescent son is "a little man now / And knows already what a whizz *he* is." The resolution of the story, perhaps a bit too pat for what precedes, has her pondering whether to show the world what a whizz she really can be by transposing a few figures and opening "an account in another name in another bank / In another part of town." If they catch her after her retirement or death, they will ask "What need had she to do it?" and "Did she never think of her son / And how it would affect him / And his future . . . ?" Ah, did she not? "She takes up her pen," we are told in the last lines of the story, "And carefully, thoughtfully, / She begins her first transposing."

The last and possibly least dramatic of the verse narratives is "Three Heroines," which suggests nothing so much as an occasional poem, commemorating as it does the last social event attended by a witty and elegant Southern grande dame at eighty-six. This final emergence of the terminally ill dowager into her country club world is a painful act of heroism in a trivial cause—a fitting farewell for a life that never called upon her "to show / Her colors" as the heroine she might have been. The narrator, the woman's fiftyish son, is suitably elegiac as he escorts his mother, listens to her reminiscences about her Civil War grandmother, and watches the faithful black maid like a tender fairy godmother remove his mother's gold lamé dress and miniature slippers and ready her for the inevitable striking of the final clock. The three heroines of the title are the aged mother, her own vain, frivolous but brave ancestor who the narrator notes seems "nearly one" with her, and the black servant who embodies the heroism of those who only stand and wait.

The "Conditions Established" by the Poet

The somewhat tenuous association of these stories with several traditional verse forms—the dramatic monologue, the ballad, the psychological character portrait, and the elegy—is hardly enough to justify Taylor's risky venture. Although the stories' meanings may be enhanced by a subtle linkage to the conventions of these poetic subgenres, expectations are created by the use of verse—even free verse—that are not satisfied by this alone. Seeing something printed as verse on the page, the reader automatically, as a kind of conditioned response, begins to look for elements not necessarily expected in prose: images that startle or provoke; feelings of some intensity and power; figures that yoke unexpected things to give new insights; language that evocatively compresses much into little; rhythms that guide and move the reader like an unheard drum.

Does Taylor in these story-poems fulfill or frustrate such expectations? Imagery is no more vivid in these stories than in his others in prose; figures of speech are no more abundant than elsewhere; emotion, where present, tends to be dramatic or narrative rather than lyrical. The language seems to hurry no more, condense no more, intensify no more than is Taylor's usual practice. Here, just as Anatole Broyard has observed about Taylor's long prose stories, "striking effects of language, imagery, or style are disdained as if by definition. Homeliness is a virtue."[10]

Rhythm is all that is left that might be the compelling reason for the experiment. But it is easy to see that the meter is basically free—no set lengths to lines, no prescribed number of feet, no necessary pattern of stresses or accents. If there is an iambic feel to many of the lines, it is no more pronounced than in most nonmetrical prose. Passages from some of the other stories originally written in verse format but printed as prose could be easily reconstituted in broken lines such as these, but we could never be sure we made the breaks where Taylor had intended them. Take, for example, the beginning of "The Captain's Son," which in its printed form in *In the Miro District* looks like this:

> There is an exchange between the two cities of Nashville and Memphis which has been going on forever—for two centuries almost. (That's forever in Tennessee.) It's like this: A young man of good family out at Memphis, for whom something has gone wrong, will often take up residence in Nashville. And of course it works the other way around. (*IMD,* 5)

It can readily be recast as free verse like this:

> There is an exchange
> Between the two cities of Nashville and Memphis
> Which has been going on forever—
> For two centuries almost.
> (That's forever in Tennessee.)
> It's like this: A young man of good family
> Out at Memphis, for whom something has gone wrong,
> Will often take up residence in Nashville.
> And of course it works the other way around.

The metrical line divisions, whatever else they may do or not do, control the reader's perception of the syntactic and rhetorical structures of the sentences.

But they control them in only one of many possible ways. Suppose the lines had been divided like this:

> There is an exchange between the two cities
> Of Nashville and Memphis which has been going on
> Forever—for two centuries almost. (That's
> Forever in Tennessee.) It's like this:
> A young man of good family out at Memphis, for whom
> Something has gone wrong, will often take up
> Residence in Nashville. And of course it works
> The other way around.

The rearrangement focuses attention on elements that would get less attention with alternative breakings of the lines.

What Taylor controls more fully in his verse narratives than in his prose narratives then is verbal structure. Through the line divisions he shapes the phrases and clauses in units of his own choosing and we are led to hear his words not as we might naturally arrange them, but as the prosody has arranged them for us.

That advantage may not be worth the risk of creating other generic expectations that are left unfulfilled. But if those other generic expectations are minimal in the fiction-reading audience, Taylor may have achieved a new kind of control of reader response with little undesired side effect. As Northrop Frye has observed, "the genre is determined by the conditions established between the poet and the public."[11] Peter Taylor just may have established the conditions that permit him to crack the genre barrier and that set up for him the hybrid form most congenial to his special artistic goals.

The Return to "Regular Prose Form"

The two new stories in *The Old Forest* (a volume that also reassembled eleven stories and *The Death of a Kinsman* from previous collections) and four of the remaining six stories in *In the Miro District* were also originally written, according to Taylor himself, in the broken-line format. But Taylor has acknowledged the difficulty of maintaining the verselike attention to structure and intensity in the longer, more complex stories:

> I write first in that way because it makes me give a lot more attention to the interest of the line and the phrase. But if it gets very long and the line length—the breaking of the line—seems to have no significance, then I reconvert. Sometimes when I get to

the end of the story, I get exhausted trying to give intrinsic interest to each line. But I'll go and finish it that way. . . . If the stories bog down—and I can usually realize it—then I put them in regular prose form.[12]

Once the story is converted back to prose form, however, the question of its original verse structure becomes moot because there is no practical way for the reader to reconstruct the preferred line divisions with any certainty. And since even the stories left in verse format exhibit few hallmarks of poetry beyond the measured lines, there would seem to be little reason to approach these long prose-format stories as anything other than ordinary prose narratives, regardless of what we know of the creative process behind them.

At any rate, the two earliest stories in *In the Miro District*—"The Throughway" (1964) and "Daphne's Lover" (1969)—apparently preceded Taylor's versifying phase and began their lives in the same prose form in which they are currently printed. "The Throughway" differs in several other ways from the other new prose stories of Taylor's last two collections: it is the only story not told by a first-person narrator, the only story in which the principal characters are not affluent members of the gentry, and the only story in which noblesse oblige is neither a primary nor a secondary theme. As the account of the contradictory reactions of an old couple when their house is condemned to make way for highway construction, "The Throughway" is remarkable for its avoidance of the expected sentimental clichés. Compared to this story, in fact, "Miss Leonora When Last Seen," which concerned a similar dispossession by the right of eminent domain, might appear quite conventional and almost maudlin. In "The Throughway" Taylor goes to great pains to strip his situation of those possibilities that might give it undue social significance. Unlike Miss Leonora, Harry and Irene are nobodies, and they do not in any ostensible way represent any tradition or any historic values. Even the house they are losing is rented, not inherited or even earned by work and sacrifice. The house, moreover, is not a thing of beauty, of economic worth, or of emotional attachment. The story obviously, then, cannot be the expected melodrama about old values being crowded out by new.

The conflict in "The Throughway," in fact, is not even between the old couple and the forces of progress, but within the couple, between the husband and wife. For it is only Harry who opposes the throughway; Irene readily accepts the inevitable. As a result, they are not found as "two who [are] allied against an intruding world" but unexpectedly as "two adversaries." What Taylor focuses on in the story is the motivation that inspires the opposite reactions, the interior evaluation that each gives to the fact of dispossession. Here, again, none of the predictable explanations will unravel the mystery of why the woman cares so little about her home, or why the man cares so much. Harry and Irene themselves do not at the beginning understand their own inner reasons; and, when some understanding comes at the end, the understanding doesn't help.

By presenting the situation alternately through the consciousnesses of the two old people, Taylor commits himself to no single, simple explanation. "I own nothing," Harry says at one point. "I made up my mind early in life to ask for nothing. I thought that nothing was something they could never take away from me." But at another point, Irene insists: "Harry, my darling, all along you've wanted *everything,* which is what everybody wants—not nothing. But something inside you made you feel that it was wrong." All that can be safely said is that the issue is one of success and failure as related to ownership. But it is through that issue that "the world" comes in and estranges human being from human being, even husband from wife. And that mysterious estrangement is the fate to which Harry and Irene must turn, at the story's end, in "awful resignation."

"Daphne's Lover," like the play *The Early Guest* and the still-uncollected story "A Cheerful Disposition,"[13] features Frank Lacy as a central character; it is also therefore a remnant of the 1960s novel Taylor synopsized in *The Early Guest* and then destroyed. In this story Frank is not yet the much-married Manhattanite "in the vanguard of modern life," but just a youth in his early teens trying out his own seductive charm on the opposite sex in depression-era Memphis (not unlike the fictional Paxton of *The Early Guest*). Although Frank is at the center of the action, the real story is that of the narrator, his less venturesome boyhood friend, who has a near-voyeuristic interest in Frank's success with girls. The story's title refers in one sense to Frank, who can woo and win even an elusive Daphne, but also to the narrator, who would not presume to touch the nymph he loves lest his touch, like that of the unwelcome Apollo, should "turn her into some vegetable or leafy shrub about which [he] would have no feeling."

The Daphne/Apollo allusion epitomizes the story's theme about Southern sexual and social codes, a theme that crops up frequently in these late stories. The narrator comes from a family governed by rules, even at the card table, where "members of the opposite sexes were never allowed to be partners in bridge or to play on the same side in any game." The narrator, therefore, has thoroughly internalized a code that sets off as too sacred to touch any girl idealized either as an emblem of feminine beauty or as a prospective marriage partner. Frank, on the other hand, who comes from a family without apparent discipline, genially insinuates himself into the narrator's family for what seems the express purpose of testing and bending the rules—in cards, in domestic order, and, ultimately, in sexual conduct. Despite the fact that they are "plainly such different types," Frank and the narrator are linked by the common conviction that "if one has any imagination whatsoever, one has always to participate to some degree in the experience of one's friends." Thus "Daphne's Lover" leads into a second major theme that is also prominent in a number of the late stories: the theme of vicarious experience. Reflecting back, the now middle-aged narrator observes how he "needed to participate more wholeheartedly in the lives of others" once he knew what his own life was going to be. "I tell myself," he says, "that a healthy imagination is like a healthy appetite and must be fed. If you do not feed it the lives of your friends, I maintain, then you are apt to feed it your own life, to live in your imagination rather than upon it."

"The Gift of the Prodigal" from *The Old Forest* picks up the same themes of social/sexual codes and vicarious experience and develops them from a different perspective. The first-person narrator is here a widowed father contemplating his complex relationship with his youngest son, Ricky, a twenty-nine-year-old thrice-married ne'er-do-well. Ricky's three older siblings think that he ought not to burden his father "with his outrageous and sometimes sordid affairs," and as Ricky comes home one morning for another bail-out by his father, the father himself momentarily considers phoning one of the other children "to come and protect [him] from this monster of a son and from whatever sort of trouble he [is] now in." Instead, though, the father recalls in vivid detail a number of Ricky's prior scrapes, including a horse-dealing scam, a cockfight operation, and a shooting of a rival for his married lover's affections. The father, who has "never looked at another woman" since the day he married, seems particularly fascinated with Ricky's women: "a certain low sort" with whom he frequently consorts, another type of "intense and restless-looking" girls that he has always "gone for," and even his wives who came "from good families," yet "tended to dress themselves in a way that [the father's] own daughters wouldn't."

Despite Ricky's constant violation of the mores of his family and of his class and despite his continuing imposition on his father's mercies, the father is "wild with anticipation" to hear Ricky's latest escapade and recognizes "that it is not, after all, such a one-sided business," this business between father and son. "Whatever it will be, I know it is all anyone in the world can give me now—perhaps the most anyone has ever been able to give a man like me," the father thinks, as he urges Ricky on with his story. "I hear him beginning. I am listening," the father says, relishing the prodigal's gift of vicarious living to a parent whose own existence is circumscribed and stultified. "I am listening gratefully to all he will tell me about himself, about any life that is not my own."

The "Circumstances" of One's Birth

The title stories of *In the Miro District* and *The Old Forest,* along with the story "The Captain's Son," are perhaps the most compelling examples of Peter Taylor's storytelling at its most mature stage of development. Despite his new practice of writing first in verse format and then converting to prose typography, in technique these stories do not modify significantly the digressive-reflective memoir approach he shaped to his own individual vision and style much earlier in his career. In theme, though they mine the same lode as his earlier work, these late stories do discover rich new veins from which much narrative gold can still be extracted.

Nat Ramsey, the narrator in "The Old Forest," makes reference at one point to "the binding and molding effects upon people of the circumstances in which they were born." This theme, perhaps more than any other, Jonathan Yardley has observed, "gives Taylor's fiction its universality: no matter what world a person may be born into, his stories say, that is the world that shapes him, and this we all have in common."[14] The circumstances of birth derive from a myriad factors, but Taylor concentrates in these late stories (as indeed he has in most of his work) on the interrelated trio of region, class, and family, probing over and over again their diverse impact on various individuals. Yet, as Yardley also noted, Taylor is not defensive about any "old Southern order" implied by certain combinations of factors: he can show the same factor being destructive to one person, liberating to another.

"The Captain's Son," for instance, focuses on Tolliver Bryant Campbell, the scion of a Memphis cotton plantation family who marries into a prominent Nashville family. Three accidents of birth are critical to Tolliver's story: he comes from a Deep-South planter subculture (that has subtle but powerful differences from the subculture of his in-laws), he is too rich for his own good, and his parents are alcoholics. As we come to see Tolliver through the eyes of the narrator, his bride's younger brother, he seems pathologically passive, residing with his in-laws instead of establishing his own home, living on his wealth instead of working, and even leaving his marriage unconsummated. Eventually, the details add up to a painfully realistic portrait of what clinical counselors today refer to as "codependence" and the "adult children of alcoholics syndrome."[15] As might be expected with this background, Tolliver himself becomes a secret drinker and descends into alcoholism with his young wife in tow. At the same time, his in-laws become classic codependents

from the sense it creates of an aura of mystery about the intricacy and fragility of the ties that bind families and generations and cultures.

"The Old Forest," the longest and most complex of Peter Taylor's most recent stories, also hinges on the question of the standards governing a young Tennesseean's relationships with his own sort of girl and with girls "of a different sort." When the narrator, Nat Ramsey, has an accident on a wintry day in the 1930s with a girl of that "different sort" in the car, the stability of his whole life is momentarily placed in the direst jeopardy. The girl, Lee Ann Deehart, belongs to a group of "city girls," whom Nat and his friends "facetiously and somewhat arrogantly referred to as the Memphis demimonde," but who are really respectable, intelligent girls making their own way in respectable urban jobs and whose chief deficit is the lack of "old family connections back in the country," which give girls in Nat's social circle their presumed superior status. When Lee Ann bolts from the car following the accident and disappears into the dense woods beyond Overton Park ("the last surviving bit of the primeval forest that once grew right up to the bluffs above the Mississippi River"), she turns a trivial event into a police matter and a potential scandal that threatens Nat's engagement to his country club fiancée, Carolyn Braxley.

Of course, Taylor's familiar digressive-reflective narrative style prevents the story from being the simple unraveling of a mystery. Steven John Ross, who took on the difficult task of translating this story to film, has observed:

> As the story progresses, one of the big worries of everyone concerned is whether or not Lee Ann was hurt during the accident or has come to any harm since running off into the woods. . . . Yet Taylor has told us in the opening paragraph that the accident caused no serious injury to anyone. Moreover, the entire plot is driven by the speculation that if Lee Ann is not found Caroline will be forced to break off the engagement. Yet three pages into the story Nat . . . indirectly informs us that he did indeed marry Caroline and that they are still married forty years after the events he is describing!
>
> Clearly Taylor does not want us to be concerned with such questions as: "is she alive?"; "is she hurt?"; "will she marry him?"; "will he have the guts to dump the silly debutante and marry the working girl?" His deceptively casual and discursive style masks just how diligently he is denying us simple narrative pleasures.[17]

But Taylor has challenged conventional responses to his story in still another way. Knowing that readers would be much more ready to identify with Lee Ann, the working girl, than with Caroline, the debutante, he nevertheless "deliberately" chose the society girl for his heroine, accepting the challenge to make "a person who's normally unattractive do heroic things despite themselves and their situation." Taylor, of course, thoroughly understands Caroline's "situation" because it derives from those "binding and molding effects" of the circumstances of birth. "That's the world I knew growing up," he has said, "the world of the so-called upper class people. . . . [T]hey fascinate me. They represent an attitude toward the past that is terribly important to society."[18]

Taylor writes primarily about "so-called high society" because that is the social and cultural milieu he knows intimately enough to bring to life in authentic and credible detail. The character of Caroline Braxley is triumphant proof that a sensitive artist can find the universal even in what might seem the most elite and special environments, for Caroline emerges finally as one of the most appealing and subtly defined characters Taylor has ever created. When Nat, his father, his father's powerful friends, and the Memphis police force neither singly nor in tandem can locate the vanished Lee Ann, it is Carolyn who, without ever once compromising her genteel principles, finds the girl, solves the mystery, prevents the scandal, and salvages her impending marriage to Nat. How she does this is interesting, but why she does it comes as one of those profound insights into a time, a place, a culture, a person that distinguishes literature of the highest order. "The only power I had to save myself was to save you, and to save you by rescuing Lee Ann Deehart," Caroline tells Nat. "It always came to that, and comes to that still. Don't you see it was a question of how very much I had to lose and how little power I had to save myself. Because *I* had not set *my*self free the way those other girls have. One makes that choice at a much earlier age than this, I'm afraid. And so I knew already, Nat, and I know now what the only kind of power I can ever have must be."

Having made her commitment to "the old, country manners" her class was heir to, Caroline heroically joins that long company of Taylor characters from his earliest stories to his latest who become living representations of the frequently constraining, sometimes burdensome, often misunderstood, but always cherished values of "the old ways and the old teachings" of their birthright.

Chapter Ten

A Summons to Memphis and After

"A Story That Got Out of Hand"

In October 1986 Alfred A. Knopf announced "a crowning achievement in a distinguished career"—the publication of the "long-awaited new novel" by "one of America's finest writers." That novel was Peter Taylor's *A Summons to Memphis*. It came out four months short of a half century since the publication of Taylor's very first short story in the March 1937 issue of *River*.

Consistently over the years Taylor had eschewed the novel as the ultimate goal of a short story writer. "It used to infuriate me, the attitude that you wrote stories until you were good enough to write a novel," he told an interviewer in 1985. "I much prefer reading stories: I like James's stories better than his novels, and Faulkner's, and I think D. H. Lawrence's stories are *much* better than his novels. But people always pressure you, and it does seem like a challenge—the scope of it."[1]

Of course, Taylor had been butting up against the genre barrier for years—experimenting, as we have seen, with plays and verse narratives—and the full-length novel was the one remaining challenge he hadn't fully met. Not that he hadn't been trying all along: he published a chapter from *The Wanderer,* a novel in progress, in the Kenyon College literary magazine in 1940 when he was still a student; he published the novelette, *A Woman of Means,* in 1950; he worked five years on a novel in the sixties, eventually destroying the manuscript but synopsizing its themes in the play *The Early Guest;* he worked for some time in the seventies on a novel that was later abandoned about three first cousins born in the same month of the same year; and he has from time to time discussed various fictions in progress that could wind up either as stories or as novels.

And over the years, too, Taylor admits, "it fascinates me that my stories get longer and longer when I'm always trying to make them shorter and shorter."[2] That some of these long stories have the qualities of "miniature novels" was noted by Robert Towers in his *New York Times Book Review* critique of *The Old Forest* in 1985: "His narrative method is to hover over the action, to digress from it, to explore byways and relationships, to speculate on alternative possibilities—in short, to defy the conventions of brevity and concentration that we usually associate with the genre. What results is often a thickly populated microcosm of an entire society, with its assumptions, virtues, loyalties and snobberies revealed."[3]

If some of the published short stories are in many ways miniature novels, it is also true that *A Summons to Memphis* is in some ways an enlarged or elongated short story rather than an excursion into an altogether different form. "It's a story that got out of hand," Taylor commented while he was working on it. "And that's what a novel is for me."[4] But even though—at slightly more than two hundred pages—*A Summons to Memphis* is the longest work he has ever published, it is not significantly larger in terms of the number of characters, the complexity of the action, the span of time covered, or the depth and breadth of its themes than the major new stories in his last two story collections. It is, therefore, not so much a climactic breakthrough into a new form as it is a logical and evolutionary progression from the whole body of his work in the preceding fifty years.

"Frozen Forever in Their Roles"

The novelistic effect of *A Summons to Memphis,* to the degree that it is present at all, depends on Taylor's skillful integration of several key elements that give the book its own special color and texture. Critical to the impact any novel will have on its readers, of course, is the authenticity and appeal of the major character about whom most of the action revolves. And for that central role Taylor has created a character who is not terribly easy to like, much less love: a domineering father who appears to have wreaked irreparable damage on the lives of his family, when, in the middle of the Great Depression, he uprooted his entire household from its serene and happy existence in Nashville and deposited that same household, willy-nilly, in what seemed at the time the terribly alien culture of Memphis. The main action occurs when this widowed father at age eighty-one plans to marry again, and his two unmarried daughters summon their bachelor brother from New York to Memphis to prevent the proposed nuptials.

This father, George Carver, is in many ways an exemplar of his generation: a man of great personal attractiveness, tremendous business ability, and unquestioned integrity. A country lawyer who never forgets the values of the landed gentry from which he sprang, he rises to the top in Nashville, only to become the duped partner in the crooked financial schemes of his business partner and best friend. When the friend's betrayal is unmasked, Carver pulls up stakes and moves to the brash cotton capital of Memphis, where he builds a second fortune. Strong and righteous, forceful and determined, he is flawed only be a seeming blindness to the human toll his decisions take on his family.

At least that's the way George Carver appears to us as his story is mediated through the narration of his forty-nine-year-old son Phillip, whose knowledge of the past is dredged up from his own deeply wounded psyche and whose knowledge of the current situation is pieced together in far-off New York from the letters and phone calls of his sisters and his old school-friend Alex Mercer. As Phillip ponders his sisters' desperate pleas to him to hurry back to Memphis, he reflects on how his father, through the abrupt exiling of the family to Memphis and through other controlling actions of various sorts, has turned Phillip's mother into a virtual invalid, Phillip's brother into a death-seeking escapist who is killed in World War II, Phillip's two sisters into spinsters frozen in adolescent roles, and Phillip himself into a semireclusive Manhattan book dealer alienated to a large degree not only from his family in Memphis but from life in general.

But how reliable is Phillip as narrator? Since he holds bitter grudges not only about the traumatic migration to Memphis but about his father's deliberate obstruction of the marital plans of each of his children in turn, can he have any objectivity in regard to the past he recounts? "It's difficult to convey effectively the limitations of a narrator," Taylor confessed to a college class, but added: "I've just found a way to do that in the novel (*A Summons to Memphis*) that I'm working on."[5] He later elaborated further: "I tried telling a part of the story from the point of view of Alex Mercer, Phillip Carver's friend. But that didn't work. The whole story had to come from Phillip. What is important is his point of view and the way he goes back and forth over the years trying to understand."[6]

The other major characters of the novel are functionally foils to Phillip, forcing his attention first on one aspect of the situation, then on another. The most memorable, because the most fully realized, of these characters are the two sisters, Betsy and Josephine. Since they were twenty and nineteen respectively and had "already been brought out as young ladies in Nashville society" at the time of their transplantation to Memphis, they were not eligible by the "absolutely inviolable" rules governing debutante seasons to be presented at all in Memphis. Thus, cut off from their beaus in Nashville and never presented to the eligible young men in Memphis, they were caught in a social dilemma, the "profound significance" of which "young ladies in present-day Memphis and Nashville cannot possibly conceive." Furthermore, their only serious marriage prospects were each in turn obliquely but unequivocally rejected by their all-controlling father.

Once it became clear to them that they could have no appropriate place in Memphis society, either as postdebs on the way to the altar or as blissful young matrons, Betsy and Josephine began to live those roles that were open to them. First they were "those awful Nashville girls" with their wild ways and raucous sense of humor; then they opened their own real estate businesses and established their own independent households; finally, in their fifties, despite the fact that they still "got themselves up in the most extreme fashions that only the most sylphlike and dashing young girls should have worn in any given year," they found themselves "fully accepted as a remarkable Memphis institution." Although Betsy and Josephine perhaps had the greatest cause to resent their father, they affect an attitude of merry amusement when, shortly after their invalid mother's death, their octogenarian father first is discreetly courted by wealthy widows in his own social set and then himself begins not-so-discreetly to court wild young women in the city's less-than-respectable midtown night spots. It is only when Mr. Carver develops an attachment "to a respectable but undistinguished and schoolteacherish woman" that Betsy and Josephine prevail on their brother to help prevent their old father "from making a fatal mistake."

Phillip is indebted to Betsy and Josephine for the financial, personal, and moral support they gave him when at age thirty he made his escape from Memphis to New York, and their influence on his feelings and attitudes is not to be minimized. But Phillip does have two other influences to put some balance into his thinking. First is Alex Mercer, the old school chum from Memphis and an ardent admirer of Phillip's father, who corroborates or qualifies the information Phillip's sisters dispense, who provides a counterbalancing point of view, and who serves as a model of the filial role Phillip might have chosen to play.

Similarly influential on Phillip is Holly Kaplan, the woman in her midthirties with whom he has lived for several years in New York. Affected by her own distant relationship to her Jewish family in Cleveland, Holly tries to persuade Phillip that he must not seek revenge on his father, as his sisters were doing, but must find a way to understand him. She proposes the doctrine

> that our old people must be not merely forgiven all their injustices and unconscious cruelties in their roles as parents but that any selfishness on their parts had actually been required of them if they were to remain whole human beings and not become merely guardian robots of the young. This was something to be remembered, not

forgotten. This was something to be accepted and even welcomed, not forgotten or forgiven.[7]

"I use Holly as a comparative figure to the narrator," Taylor has said. "Her view is one way of looking at the situation. But she goes too far, and that is not the narrator's final judgment."[8]

The novel is almost two-thirds complete before we learn that Phillip will answer his summons back to Memphis. Surprisingly, his father, not his sisters, meets him at the airport—and asks him to stand up for him in his wedding that very day! As Phillip inhales "the familiar aroma of [his father's] whole life and being," he goes over again what he now feels is a profound truth:

> Forgetting the injustices and seeming injustices which one suffered from one's parents during childhood and youth must be the major part of any maturing process . . . . A certain oblivion was what we must undergo in order to become adults and live peacefully with ourselves. Suddenly my sisters seemed no longer a mystery to me. I understood much of their past conduct as never before. They were still, while actually in their mid-fifties, two little teenaged girls dressed up and playing roles. It was their way of not facing or accepting the facts of their adult life. They could not forget the old injuries. They wished to keep them alive. They were frozen forever in their roles as injured adolescents. (*STM,* 146)

But the frozen adolescents are still at work: when Phillip and his father arrive at the church they find the intended bride has changed her mind and left on a three-month trip; "events had conspired," she said, to show her their marriage could not be happy, as he "had his children to think of." The old man takes it with "a cold, bland smile." "I want to get home," he says presently, "and see what else the girls have prepared for me."

The rest of the action of the novel comes rather quickly, if somewhat anticlimactically. Betsy and Josephine abandon their own homes, move in with their father, and switch their clothing to "modest, simple housedresses," signifying they are "beginning a new life." Alex Mercer, disgusted with the whole family, leaves them all without a word. Phillip flees on the first plane out to New York. Not too long after George Carver accidentally meets his old nemesis, Lewis Shackleford, the partner who betrayed him, and is happily reconciled. The two sisters, upset anew when their father proposes to visit in Shackleford's home, issue a second emergency summons to Phillip, but Shackleford's sudden death obviates the problem. Holly, who has been separated from Phillip, rejoins him. The deaths of Holly's parents and George

Carver follow in short order. Phillip fantasizes that someday he and Holly will simply fade away without a trace, their serenity merely "translated into a serenity in another realm of being." That, Phillip thinks, is the only possible end for "two such serenely free spirits" who he says (quoting Thomas Hardy's poem "Neutral Tones") won't for a long time have been "alive enough to have the strength to die."

"Melodious Divagations"

In the course of his lengthy ruminations in his notebooks over all of this, Phillip Carver has indeed come a long way. He has developed, for instance, an admiration for what he now sees as "almost a great beauty of my father's character that from his earliest years the boy George Carver yearned for an individuality and for personal attainments that could be in no way related to the accident of his birth, longed to succeed in some realm that he had not yet heard of and could not have heard of, yearned for some mysterious achievements that could not be had on the Town Farm or on the Thorn County Courthouse square, yearned . . . 'for an otherness to everything I had been taught was mine or might be mine.'"

Yet, despite his new insights, the reader may feel that Phillip has not really penetrated the mystery of his father's personality, the full motivations of his sisters, or even the "narrowness and cowardice" of his own life. "But after all," Taylor has commented, "how successful are we ever in understanding what has happened to us? That's what I want to suggest in the novel."[9] And in *A Summons to Memphis* it is the discerning process more than the end result of the discernment that captures and intrigues the reader.

The structure of the novel is, in fact, the structure of that discernment process. Information is presented, interpreted, reviewed, reinterpreted. The same incidents are continuously alluded to and even recounted more than once, often with incremental detail, sometimes with different nuances of meaning. Some of these are major events from the past, such as the father's betrayal by Lewis Shackleford or the move to Memphis itself. Some are vivid evocations of the present consternation, such as the "amusing stories" the sisters tell about their father's night life or the calls and letters by which they summon their brother to Memphis. But too many of the reiterated details—even if not out of character for the tautological narrator—seem almost gratuitous for the purposes of the novel. If we are told on page 18 that "Jo was dark-haired and blue-eyed and much more striking-looking than Betsy," do we need to be told (by the same narrator with no discernible difference in perspective) on page 41 that "with her dark hair and blue eyes [Jo] was actually better-looking than Betsy"? If we learn on page 34 that "Father had been born" at "the old county seat of Thornton," what do we gain by being told on page 43 that Father "himself was born and bred at Thornton," on page 139 that Father "himself was of course born up there [at Thornton] in an old hip-roofed brick house," and on page 159 that "my father was born of course in that old hip-roofed brick house on the Town Farm, at Thornton"? Perhaps all this seemingly functionless redundancy is only another device to characterize an emotionally reticent but verbally garrulous narrator. Even so, the narrator's frequent self-conscious apologies ("As I have said," "As I have already explained," and variations of the same phrase) can begin to weary us as much as the information he endlessly repeats.

"Unfortunately," Robert Towers has observed, "Peter Taylor's way of circling a subject repeatedly before revealing its fictional core—a technique that contributes much to the distinctiveness of his stories—leads in the novel to prolixity and repetition"; and Walter Sullivan notes that one of Taylor's weaknesses is that "much of his work is written in the first person, and he does not always resist the temptation to self-indulgence that this point of view presents. . . . He is tedious at times."[10] John Updike, moreover, in a generally admiring review for the *New Yorker,* notes that Taylor "almost cruelly teases, with his melodious divagations and his practiced skill at foreshadowing and delaying climaxes, the reader of this novel." Updike also complains mildly not only about "narrative churning" which "brings up only what is already floating on the surface," but about "fastidious" diction, "portly" sentences, and "prissy, circuitous" language. And yet, Updike himself admits, "this language, with its echo of old usages and once-honored forms, delivers things a less quaint diction could hardly express. . . . Beneath his talky, creaking courtesies, Peter Taylor deals fascinatingly with the primal causes of the social contract."[11]

Uncollected Works and Works-in-Progress

A Summons to Memphis may indeed by in many ways just what the publishers called it: Peter Taylor's "crowning achievement." But judging from the number of stories Taylor has that are still uncollected and from the number of works he has reported in progress in recent years, it may not be the last claimant to that honor.

Some of Taylor's as yet uncollected stories will probably never be brought out in book form. Six early stories have now been passed over several times as Taylor compiled various collections and are likely candidates for oblivion. The two earliest of these—his first professional publications—were probably written while Taylor was a freshman at Southwestern at Memphis; Allen Tate sent them to the short-lived Mississippi magazine *River,* which published them in March and April 1937.[12] "The Party" introduced the subject that was to become Taylor's own special property: the migration of rural Southerners to the big city. Tinted with the sociocultural vision of the Nashville Agrarians, the story concerns a young man whose family had quit the country but who himself comes back from the city to till an inherited farm; he gives a reunion party for his urban friends to test his young wife's devotion to their country way of life. We are not surprised, however, that the wife has only had her contentment with pastoral delights restored by her contact with the city dwellers, since in detail after detail the story has depicted the rural life as leisurely, cultured, and full of sincere fellowship.

The second *River* story, "The Lady is Civilized," contains as part of its melodramatic plot the same incident of the dismemberment of a black man by his wife and lover that was to crop up twenty-two years later in "A Friend and Protector." A soap-opera subject (an ambitious wife selling herself to an old roué), belabored symbols (a picture of Judas to suggest the wife's betrayal, for instance), and an affected prose style ("The rain was beating murderously down" begins all three sentences of the first paragraph)—all these indicate an immature writer self-consciously striving for effect and are far removed from what Taylor was doing just a couple of years later.

Another early piece much inferior to the later work is "The School Girl" (1942),[13] about a little girl whose whole story is given away when Taylor describes "the single curl which was brushed down precisely in the center of the girl's forehead." Of course, when she is good she brings home a very, very good report card, but when she is bad she horridly impales a live butterfly for a bonnet decoration. "Attendant Evils," included in a 1944 Vanderbilt anthology,[14] comes close to being good Taylor material. Written as a letter of a Southern matron to her married daughter, it treats the problem of running a Southern household when one of the "attendant evils" of World War II was impudent and unreliable black help. But through between-the-lines irony and through humorous situations in which "stupid, sullen" blacks use passive defiance to frustrate the irate white woman, Taylor reveals domineering and condescending patricianism as an "attendant evil" of another war—the long-standing clash between classes and races in the South.

Taylor has publicly expressed his disaffection for several other uncollected stories. One is "Uncles," a story he dashed off for the *New Yorker* in 1949 just to be eligible for a bonus from the magazine.[15] "I was rather proud at the time to be able to do it, but then I felt a deep guilt," he says of the experience. "I didn't want to write that way, and I didn't write for them for some time."[16]

"Uncles" is about a Kenyon College freshman who, on Christmas vacation at St. Louis, realizes that the bourgeois "one-dimensional, exclusively masculine view of life" of his father and uncles rules out the artistic life he is considering: "It suddenly became clear that everything clever, gentle, and light belonged to women and the world they lived in. To men belonged only the more serious things in life, the deadly practical things—constructive ideas, profitable jobs, stories with morals, jokes with points."

Another uncollected *New Yorker* story, "Nerves" (1961), has a Nashville native back home on a visit listening to a stranger in Centennial Park launch into a "totally unexpected" and "quite remarkable" monologue about changes that have taken place in the city since his childhood.[17] Symbolizing the changes are the various means of public transportation used in different eras: first mule cars, then streetcars, now buses. The stranger captures each epoch in little vignettes illustrative of prevailing social attitudes—with contemporary mores summed up by an interracial conflict on a bus, as shocking as "a wirephoto from some scene of trouble on the other side of the world."

Taylor has also referred to "some bad stories" in the *Sewanee Review* and other magazines that he wrote "with a theory." "I didn't really have anything to write," he has said, "and I got heavily symbolic—things that I don't really have much sympathy with."[18] It is likely that he was alluding to "A Cheerful Disposition" and "Tom, Tell Him" in *Sewanee Review* and "The End of Play" in *Virginia Quarterly Review*.[19] "A Cheerful Disposition" features Frank Lacy, a character from Taylor's aborted sixties novel, who also appears in "Daphne's Lover" and *The Early Guest*. Now an aging New Yorker returning to his hometown for the funeral of his eldest brother (the first family member of his generation to die), Frank, who prides himself on his "cheerful disposition," at first is pleased by the familiarity of the attendant rituals, but winds up with a terrifying dream in which he sees himself in his brother's coffin. This dream, "born of being home," convinces him that home can mean "a glimpse of childhood" no longer; home is now forevermore a confrontation with mortality, the ultimate devastation wrought by the changes of time. "Tom, Tell Him" comes the closest of any Taylor story to having a religious subject: it is based on actual episodes in Trenton (here called Blackwell) involving the demolition of an abandoned Episcopal church and the conversion of its old baptismal font into a birdbath by the redneck demolition contractor.[20] But the real subject is not religion at all, but the loss of one more "relic from the past" and the ambivalence of feelings about the loss. The narration is so pedestrian, however, and the handling of the central conflict so oblique that the story hardly meets Taylor's usual standard of excellence.

"The End of Play" is one more Taylor memoir story, set this time in St.

Louis in the presidential campaign summer of 1932, when the narrator (then eleven years old) was playing his own invented "Convention game," creating fantasy delegates in imitation of the nominating conventions he had listened to on the radio. One such fictive product of the boy's game is a delegate from Tennessee—"a sort of Senator Claghorn created ten years or so before the radio reproduced him"—who becomes a persona through which the boy can attempt communication, both belligerent and conciliatory, with his father, who is trying to overcome the boy's ambivalent feelings toward a possible move back to the family's ancestral hometown of Thornton. When the father-son conflict on this issue expends itself, there is an "end of play"—an end to the Convention game but also an end to all the childish "fantasies and play-pretends" the boy had hitherto been wont to engage in. "The End of Play" is structurally and thematically interesting, but like most of these other uncollected stories it apparently never took on enough life of its own to satisfy completely its demanding author.

Another group of uncollected works are five "broken-line prose" pieces from Taylor's versifying phase of the 1970s. Three of these were published in *Ploughshares,* one in the British magazine *Agenda,* and one in both *Ploughshares* and *Agenda.*[21] "Peachtrees Gone Wild in the Lane" is the shortest (only twenty-three lines) and the most lyrical: a sensuous response to a walk in a lost lane in an "innocent, wild garden," with the speaker "imagining or merely pretending" to be "young, innocent, excited and gone wild again." "Five Miles from Home" is a little longer (eighty-nine lines) and more didactic than lyrical, as barn swallows seem to warn a wanderer in a "half forgotten countryside" not to try to "prettify and destroy with your nostalgia."

The others are more obviously stories, similar to those in verse format in *In the Miro District.* "His Other Life" has the same French setting and some of the same overtones as "*Je Suis Perdu*": a father moving his family out of their Paris apartment for their return to America goes back for his hat, enters by mistake the wrong apartment, and indulges momentarily in a fantasy of a second life with a French wife and French children. "Knowing" recounts a World War II parachutist's awareness during a descent over a Dutch tulip field in enemy territory that he already knew even then "what the life *was* I was not going to have / If I didn't survive / What it would be *like.*" "We know nothing and everything from the beginning," the parachutist thinks. "The day we are born / It's all there."

"The Megalopolitans," at ten pages, has more space to develop some favorite Taylor themes. Beginning with a Boston mayor's comment ("In some ways Boston / Is every American's city") as an epigraph, "The Megalopolitans" is a series of reflections on what Boston meant to the speaker's grandfather, great-grandfather, and uncle and what it now means to the speaker as he is mugged during a 2 A.M. walk near Harvard Square. "Who cares about Boston?" the speaker says. "The whole of it / Is but the north end / Of the strip coming up from Washington / We call Megalopolis." And the gang of muggers in "slick jackets" and "tight pants" are "the true denizens of Megalopolis"; they at least preserve some of the distinctions the rest of the world has lost: "It's not all one with *them*—not by a long shot." The broken-line prose format works here perhaps better than in any other Taylor "stoem," and "The Megalopolitans" certainly deserves Ashley Brown's designation as the "small masterpiece" of Taylor's newly devised poetic medium, if not Brown's further claim that it is "the most powerful thing Mr. Taylor has ever written."[22]

In addition to the possibility of a new volume compiling some of Taylor's still uncollected works, there is also the hopeful prospect that some of the works reported in progress over the past few years will eventually be presented to the public. Certainly, one of the most interesting-sounding of these is a novel last mentioned as entitled *To the Lost State* (an allusion to the state of Franklin, which was formed in the area that is now Tennessee, but which never got admitted to the Union).[23] The central situation occurs in 1915 on a train bringing a U.S. senator's body from Washington to Tennessee for burial. Characters in the cortege include three daughters of the senator in one drawing room, their widowed stepmother and aunt in another, and in between men relatives (some of whom are getting drunk). On board also is the senator's nephew, a country boy in love with all three of the senator's daughters, whom Taylor describes as an antimacho hero who suffers because he is a family outsider and whom we also see as a peculiar old bachelor in the 1970s. The narrator, the senator's grandson, was not himself a passenger on the train, but has heard about the fabled event all his life; he fills in the background for one hundred years before the train ride and traces the lives and marriages of the three sisters up to the near-present. *To the Lost State* will surely be a Taylor tour de force.

Other works that have been reported in progress include: a novel about three first cousins born in the same month of the same year; a play about the fathers and grandfathers of these three first cousins; two novels and two plays with the same mountain resort setting as *A Stand in the Mountains;* a play about two old widows who have spent most of their lives taking girls to Europe; a story about people who leave a town and become something quite different (like the Stanhopes in Trollope); and sketches of literary people Taylor has known. Of course, some of these works have no doubt already been aborted, merged, or subsumed under something else. But despite the illnesses that have afflicted Taylor in recent years, there is plenty of reason to think his publishing career is far from finished.

"To Assert the Universality of Our Experience"

It was Robert Penn Warren who over forty years ago, through his introduction to *A Long Fourth,* presented the promising new writer Peter Taylor to the world: a brilliant young man with "a disenchanted mind, but a mind that nevertheless understands and values enchantment." It is Warren also who has provided the best thumbnail sketch of the Peter Taylor we know today: "the splendid, beautiful, cunning writer, who has made a certain segment of American life his own forever, who writes stories that are singularly and subtly his own, and who lately has been writing another kind of story which I find very exciting and perhaps revolutionary." "If I had to name the few writers of our century who have captured a true and original world in the story form," Warren goes on, "I should have Peter's name very high on a very short list."[24]

Indeed, Peter Taylor's achievement is seldom disputed these days. Although it took some time for the quiet power of his work to be recognized, that work is now seen as providing a whole new dimension to the fabled Southern Renaissance. As Louis D. Rubin, Jr., has pointed out: "The South that Faulkner, Wolfe, Tate, Ransom, and their contemporaries knew when they were growing up in the years before the First World War was vastly different from the South between the wars."[25] As part of the generation that grew up in the thirties and forties, Taylor thus writes out of a different experience than the Southern literary luminaries who were his models and mentors. But as a Southerner who spent his formative years in progressive urban centers of both the South and the Midwest, he also writes out of an experience different even from that of most of his Southern contemporaries.

Perhaps because of his different vantage point, Taylor never picked up the characteristics that we associate with that amorphous "Southern School" that flourished in the forties and fifties. "Violence dominates Southern fiction written since 1930," Louise Gossett has argued with ample justification,[26] but it certainly has not dominated Taylor's work. Where violence does appear (as in "A Friend and Protector," "An Overwhelming Question," or "The Gift of the Prodigal"), it is muted, not exploited; "The Hand of Emmagene," with its balladlike folk quality, is one of the few stories to contain vivid violence at its very center. Only a couple of the plays (*Arson* and *A Stand in the Mountains*) have any violence that is halfway sensational—and all of that occurs offstage or is suggested just at curtain close! Gothic settings and grotesque characters are equally rare; the stories where they do occur (like "A Spinster's Tale" or "Venus, Cupid, Folly, and Time") are decided deviations from the typical Taylor fare.

In his style, too, Taylor has little affinity with either the fancy flights of rhetoric that make some Southern writers sound like Jefferson Davis Day orators, or the raw, earthy, frontier-type humor that dominates works like Faulkner's *The Hamlet* and Eudora Welty's *The Robber Bridegroom*. Though his grandfather and great-uncle, Governor Bob and Governor Alf Taylor, were both highly articulate rhetoricians, as well as practitioners of folksy tall-tale comedy, and though Taylor himself was well steeped in the oral tradition of the South, he generally chooses to write in the cool, classically simple, urbane style of people far removed from the bucolic background that made such rhetoric and such humor possible.

Despite these departures from some of the standard features of the so-called Southern school, Taylor does in many ways reveal his kinship to his fellow writers in the Southern Renaissance. He has, first of all, that all-important sense of "place" that seems to color the whole sensibility of a Southerner. "Place can focus the gigantic, voracious eye of genius, and bring its gaze to point," Eudora Welty has said.[27] Taylor's eye is indeed focused by place, but it is not focused on quite the expected point. Whereas the usual Southern writer zooms in on either the anachronistic plantation home or the fading country town, Taylor almost completely avoids the first and uses the second primarily as the remembered background of his urban characters. Although the country town is only occasionally the actual setting of a story, it is very frequently a dominating symbol in the lives of characters who derived their inherited codes of manners and mores from it. The conflicts Taylor's characters face in the roles they seem constrained to play most often come from the mismatch between these idealized and old-fashioned codes and roles and the pragmatic, modern milieu in which they now live.

Taylor also shares the typical Southern preoccupation with history, tradition, and change. Even here, however, his attitude toward the subject represents a significant shift: his tone is not so much nostalgic as it is ironic. When he creates characters who yearn for a return to past values (Uncle Jake in "The Scoutmaster" or Miss Patty Bean in "Their Losses"), he presents the characters and their opinions objectively from an external point of view. Even if the tone of a story as a whole is sympathetic to the character's ideas, Taylor offers certain small contrasts to provide ironic qualification. Thus, he may not make fun of Miss Leonora in "Miss Leonora When Last Seen" or Aunt Munsie in "What You Hear from 'Em?" to the point of satire, but he does direct our attention to details that prevent us from accepting wholeheartedly the philosophic position of the character.

"The role of Southern literature," Taylor has argued, "has, in some measure, been to discover how we are different and perhaps to assert our difference. But equally and simultaneously it has been to assert the universality of our experience. And that is the nature and concern of all literature. The theme of any profound work of art is to be found in the relation of the particular to the general, the particular to the universal."[28]

His own use of the Southern experience in his work is the best proof that the most exactingly particular fiction can indeed bring the reader in touch with the universals of human thought and feeling.

"The Emotions of Recognition"

However delightful some of the individual effects are in his two novels and his several plays, Peter Taylor's achievement is linked primarily to one specific form: the short story. Not only is the bulk of his canon in this form, the best of his work—the most satisfying and the most profound—is also in this form.

"Paradox has characterized the development of the short story in America," William Peden, one of the foremost experts on the genre, has asserted. Peden's point is that, "although it is the only major literary form of essentially American origin and the only one in which American writers have always tended to excel, it has for decades been considered a parvenu, and until very recently most critics have refused to consider it as important as the more traditional forms of poetry, drama, and the novel."[29] The paradox of Peter Taylor's delayed recognition is part of this more general paradox involving the short story as a genre.

Taylor has compared himself to Anthony Trollope, and his position in the history of the twentieth-century American short story is indeed analogous to that of Trollope in the history of the nineteenth-century English novel. "There are two kinds of taste in the appreciation of imaginative literature: the taste for emotions of surprise, and the taste for emotions of recognition," Henry James noted in his essay on Trollope. "It is the latter that Trollope gratifies, and he gratifies it the more that the medium of his own mind, through which we see what he shows us, gives a confident direction to our sympathy."[30] Peter Taylor gratifies this same taste for emotions of recognition, and he gratifies it through much the same method that James attributes to Trollope—through his "complete appreciation of the usual." Another way of putting it would be to say that Taylor takes the commonplace subject matter of a William Dean Howells and runs it through the rarefied mind of a Henry James.

In neither technique nor theme is Taylor likely to seem startling or disturbing. Only in a few stories does he try such self-conscious techniques as dramatic monologue ("A Walled Garden," "The Instruction of a Mistress"), montage structure ("Sky Line"), present-tense narration ("Allegiance"), bawdy humor ("Reservations"), or allegory ("Venus, Cupid, Folly, and Time," "Miss Leonora When Last Seen"). On the other hand, he has experimented frequently with his "broken-line prose" narratives or "stoems" and with a revival of the ghost story as a serious genre ("A Strange Story," the seven plays in *Presences, The End of Play*). Nowhere does Taylor employ the sordid or morbid subject matter, the disjunctive structure and style, the abstruse symbolism, or the scatological diction characteristic of so many of his colleagues in contemporary fiction. He is never brutal, coarse, shocking; but neither is he precious, coy, titillating. The voice that speaks in his stories is essentially the voice of a gentleman—cultured but not dilettantish, ironic but not cynical, urbane but not foppish, sensitive but not sentimental. In short, Taylor preserves what was best in the genteel tradition in American letters, without any of the mawkishness and prudery often associated with it.

Taylor's subjects and themes, like his techniques, neither exploit nor affront popular taste. There is little that is daring, iconoclastic, or revolutionary in what Peter Taylor has to say. To note this characteristic, however, is not to say that he is banal or platitudinous. Limiting himself artistically to a relatively narrow range of experience, Taylor nevertheless probes deeply within this circumscribed area, preferring generally to make a refinement on an old idea rather than to propose a totally new one. "And he has always been content to use his material; he never argues about it," Walter Sullivan has observed.[31] His own philosophic position seems one of mild, gentlemanly skepticism: skepticism about the validity for the present day of social and cultural values we have inherited from our past, and skepticism about the vacuum of values that results when old values are repudiated and new ones have not been developed to take their place. Like Chekhov, Taylor is more inclined to try to state questions correctly than to attempt definitive answers. His "disenchanted mind" that "understands and values enchantment" (to use Warren's terms again) neither builds up new castles in the air from his own fancies, nor tears down those built by others. He has the rare gift of being able to criticize and appreciate simultaneously, to mix nostalgia and irony in a compound that retains the piquancy of both.

"I consider the fiction I have written merely a by-product of my efforts to understand who and what I am," Taylor has said.[32] And in the pursuit of this task he has accomplished two quite remarkable things. He has found a way, through his digressive-reflective memoir technique, to provide even within the restrictive confines of a short story a richness and density and complexity of experience that is rare enough even in the much larger scope of the novel. And he has given life to that experience in a gallery of unforgettable characters who are the glory of his art. Uncle Jake, Josie Carlson, Harriet Wilson, Sylvia Harrison, Aunt Munsie, the Tolliver family, Jess McGeehee, Miss Leonora Logan, Matt Donelson, Grandfather Manley, and Caroline Braxley—these are the proof of Henry James's dictum that "we care what happens to people only in proportion as we know what people are."[33] "In the final analysis," William Peden has aptly said, "Taylor's fiction is meaningful because his characters are meaningful."[34]

In an age when alienation seems to be man's all-too-frequent lot, Peter Taylor offers a quiet hope and consolation. When we read his stories (and his novels and plays), we are gently reassured that humankind has not yet completely lost the capacity to know and, on occasion, to love. As much or more than any other writer of our day he has brought to life in his work what he himself has described as the literary legacy of his region: "a sense of humor, a sense of character, a sense of history, a sense of the mystery of life."[35]

Notes and References

Preface

1. Wendy Smith, "*PW* Interviews: Peter Taylor," in *Conversations with Peter Taylor,* ed. Hubert H. McAlexander (Jackson: University Press of Mississippi, 1987), 64, hereafter cited as *Conversations.*

2. For representative comments of reviewers see *Contemporary Literary Criticism* (Detroit: Gale Research, 1973–1986), vols. 1, 4, 18, 39, and 44.

3. "*Esquire*'s Guide to the Literary Universe," *Esquire,* August 1987, 56.

4. Barbara Thompson, "Interview with Peter Taylor," in *Conversations,* 154.

Chapter One

1. *Literature, Sewanee, and the World* (Sewanee, Tenn.: University of the South, 1972), [3]. Biographical information for this chapter has been compiled from Taylor's published articles; standard biographical and critical reference works; interviews and newspaper accounts; press releases; notes on contributors in magazines; biographies, letters, and reminiscences from Taylor's friends and associates; materials from the Kenyon College archives and the University of Virginia news office; and letters of Taylor to the author.

2. "Tennessee Caravan, 1920–1940," in *Tennessee: A Homecoming,* ed. John Netherton (Nashville: Third National Corp., 1985), 64. Cf. similar descriptions in "The Dark Walk" and *A Summons to Memphis.*

3. "The End of Play," *Virginia Quarterly Review* 41 (Spring 1965): 264–65.

4. Hubert H. McAlexander, "A Composite Conversation with Peter Taylor," in *Conversations,* 121.

5. Don H. Doyle, *Nashville in the New South, 1880–1930* (Knoxville: University of Tennessee Press, 1985), 226, 231.

6. J. William Broadway, "A Conversation with Peter Taylor," in *Conversations,* 98. See also McAlexander, "Composite Conversation," 119, and James Curry Robison, "Interview, 1987," in James Curry Robison, *Peter Taylor: A Study of the Short Fiction* (Boston: Twayne Publishers, 1988), 136.

7. "Uncles," *New Yorker,* 17 December 1949, 28.

8. Thompson, "Interview," 156.

9. Ibid., 141.

10. Ibid., 141–42.

11. Such stories would include "Two Ladies in Retirement," "The Dark Walk," "The Other Times," "Promise of Rain," "The Little Cousins," "A Strange Story," "Daphne's Lover," "Uncles," and "End of Play."

12. Robert Brickhouse, "Peter Taylor: Writing, Teaching, and Making Discoveries," in *Conversations,* 50; McAlexander, "Composite Conversation," 116.

13. Allen Tate, "Peter Taylor," *Shenandoah* 28, no. 2 (Winter 1977):10.

14. "Biographical Notes," in *The House of Fiction,* ed. Caroline Gordon and Allen Tate (New York: Charles Scribner's Sons, 1950), 648.

15. Stephen Goodwin, "An Interview with Peter Taylor," in *Conversations,* 7. See also Broadway, "Conversation," 82.

16. McAlexander, "Composite Conversation," 118; Robert Daniel, "The Inspired Voice of Mythical Tennessee," in *Conversations,* 44.

17. "Reminiscences," in *The Fugitives, the Agrarians, and Other Twentieth Century Southern Writers* (Charlottesville: Alderman Library, University of Virginia, 1985), 18.

18. See Ian Hamilton, *Robert Lowell: A Biography* (New York: Random House, 1982); Mary Jarrell, ed., *Randall Jarrell's Letters* (Boston: Houghton Mifflin, 1985); Jean Stafford, "Some Letters to Peter and Eleanor Taylor," *Shenandoah* 30, no. 3 (Spring 1970):27–55; Robert Lowell, Peter Taylor, and Robert Penn Warren, eds., *Randall Jarrell, 1914–1965* (New York: Farrar, Straus, & Giroux, 1967).

19. Eleanor Taylor's works include *Wilderness of Ladies* (1960), *Welcome Eumenides* (1972), and *New and Selected Poems* (1983).

20. "Acceptance by Peter Taylor," *Proceedings* (American Academy and Institute of Arts and Letters), 2d ser., no. 29 (1979):31.

21. Thompson, "Interview," 158–59. See also Robison, "Interview," 138.

22. Brickhouse, "Writing, Teaching," 52.

23 Michael Kernan, "Peter Taylor and the Layers of Life," *Washington Post,* 4 March 1985, B6.

24. Robison, "Interview," 145.

Chapter Two

1. *A Long Fourth and Other Stories* (New York: Harcourt, Brace, 1948); hereafter cited as *LF.*

2. Also in *The Old Forest and Other Stories* (Garden City, N.Y.: Dial Press [Doubleday], 1985), 271; hereafter cited as *OF.*

3. Also in *Miss Leonora When Last Seen and Fifteen Other Stories* (New York: Ivan Obolensky, 1963), 102–3; hereafter cited as *ML.*

4. Also in *The Collected Stories of Peter Taylor* (New York: Farrar, Straus & Giroux, 1969), 154; hereafter cited as *CS.*

5. Goodwin, "Interview," 10–11; Broadway, "Conversation," 79–80.

6. Oswald Spengler, *The Decline of the West,* trans. Charles Francis Atkinson (New York: Alfred A. Knopf, 1961), 2:327–29.

7. Ibid., 165.

Chapter Three

1. Goodwin, "Interview," 17.

2. *A Woman of Means* (New York: Harcourt, Brace, 1950). All citations are to the recent hardcover reprint (New York: Frederic C. Beil, 1983); hereafter cited as *WM.*

3. Kenneth Clay Cathey, "Peter Taylor: An Evaluation," *Western Review* 18 (Autumn 1953):16–17.

Chapter Four

1. *The Widows of Thornton* (New York: Harcourt, Brace, 1954); hereafter cited as *WT.*

2. "Mr. Taylor's Widows," *Kenyon Alumni Bulletin* 12, no. 1 (Winter 1954):4. Most of this quotation is also reprinted on the dust jacket of *WT.*

3. Eudora Welty, "Place in Fiction," in *The Eye of the Story: Selected Essays and Reviews* (New York: Random House, 1978), 122, 121.

4. "The Dark Walk" probably best reveals the original plan of *WT,* but it is the only story in the collection that Taylor has never reprinted in another volume. "I have never thought it a success as a story," he says (correspondence with author 30 August 1988).

Chapter Five

1. Cathey, "Evaluation," 14–18.

2. *The Death of a Kinsman: A Play, Sewanee Review* 58 (Winter 1949):86–119.

3. Goodwin, "Interview," 18.

4. Brainard Cheney, "Peter Taylor's Plays," *Sewanee Review* 70 (Autumn 1962):580.

5. Cathey, "Evaluation," 15.

6. Morgan Blum, "Peter Taylor: Self-Limitation in Fiction," *Sewanee Review* 70 (Autumn 1962):560.

7. *Tennessee Day in St. Louis: A Comedy* (New York: Random House, 1957); hereafter cited as *TD.*

8. Compare the parents in "The Scoutmaster" who play cards at the peak of a family crisis.

Chapter Six

1. *Happy Families Are All Alike* (New York: McDowell, Obolensky, 1959); hereafter cited as *HF.*

2. McAlexander, "Composite Conversation," 120; Broadway, "Conversation," 113.

3. Blum, "Self-Limitation," 567–68.

4. Broadway, "Conversation," 77.

5. Cathey, "Evaluation," 10; Blum, "Self-Limitation," 562.

6. Brickhouse, "Writing, Teaching," 52.

7. Katherine Anne Porter, "Notes on Writing," in *The Collected Essays and Occasional Writings of Katherine Anne Porter* (New York: Delacorte Press, 1970), 449.

8. Jenice Jordan, "He 'Writes for Fun,' but His Stories Sell," *Columbus Dispatch,* 6 December 1959, book section.

9. The "battle" imagery is discussed by Sister Cor Mariae Schuler, "The House of Peter Taylor: Fiction and Structure" (Ph.D. diss., University of Notre Dame, 1964), 244. See also Thompson, "Interview," 143.

10. Taylor began "Heads of Houses" as a re-creation of an actual humorous incident, but "had to dump a complete draft" when he decided to concentrate on Henry Parker, the brother-in-law, throwing out the ending that had been his original inspiration. See Goodwin, "Interview," 9–10; Broadway, "Conversation," 80–81; Thompson, "Interview," 143–44.

11. Jordan, "'Writes for Fun,'" book section.

12. Thompson, "Interview," 157–58. See also Goodwin, "Interview," 12, 16; McAlexander, "Composite Conversation," 120, 122.

13. For various critical insights into "Venus, Cupid, Folly, and Time," see: Alan Williamson, "Identity and the Wider Eros: A Reading of Peter Taylor's Stories," *Shenandoah* 30, no. 1 (Fall 1978):78–80; David Robinson, "Tennessee, Taylor, the Critics, and Time," *Southern Review* 23, no. 2 (April 1987):281–94; Marilyn Malina, "An Analysis of Peter Taylor's 'Venus, Cupid, Folly, and Time,'" *Studies in Short Fiction* 20, no. 4 (Fall 1983):249–54.

14. Two potentially grotesque characters in "The Other Times"—the toothless three-hundred-pound tavern owner and her deaf-mute husband—become credibly realistic in Taylor's understated treatment.

15. Thompson, "Interview," 157.

Chapter Seven

1. Goodwin, "Interview," 12.

2. Ibid., 12, 16; McAlexander, "Composite Conversation," 126; Thompson, "Interview," 155–56, 171.

3. McAlexander, "Composite Conversation," 119.

Chapter Eight

1. Goodwin, "Interview," 21.

2. Ibid., 18.

3. Daniel, "Inspired Voice," 46, and Edwin Howard, "Writer Peter Taylor Is Home," in *Conversations,* 5. See also Goodwin, "Interview," 19.

4. Goodwin, "Interview," 20.

5. *A Stand in the Mountains* (New York: Frederic C. Beil, 1985), originally published in *Kenyon Review* 30, no. 2 (1968):169–264; hereafter cited as *SIM*.

6. McAlexander, "Composite Conversation," 123.

7. Broadway, "Conversation," 97–98. See also *SIM,* 107.

8. Thompson, "Interview," 168.

9. *Presences: Seven Dramatic Pieces* (Boston: Houghton Mifflin, 1973); hereafter cited as *PSDP.*

10. Goodwin, "Interview," 18.

11. Quoted in publisher's blurb on inside front cover of *PSDP.*

12. Taylor has acknowledged that *Missing Person* is an unconscious "steal" from Henry James's "The Jolly Corner" (Broadway, "Conversation," 99; Thompson, "Interview," 148–49).

13. *The Early Guest, Shenandoah* 24, no. 2 (Winter 1973):21–43. Reprinted as a limited edition chapbook (Winston-Salem: Palaemon Press, 1982).

14. Thompson, "Interview," 161–62.

15. Ibid., 162.

16. Ibid.

Chapter Nine

1. *In the Miro District and Other Stories* (New York: Alfred A. Knopf, 1977); hereafter cited as *IMD.*

2. See chapter 10 for a discussion of these stories.

3. Thompson, "Interview," 160–61.

4. Daniel, "Inspired Voice," 44.

5. Thompson, "Interview," 166.

6. Ibid., 161.

7. Daniel, "Inspired Voice," 45.

8. Keith Cushman, review of *In the Miro District, Studies in Short Fiction* 14, no. 4 (Fall 1977):420. But according to Robert Wilson, Introduction to *In the Miro District,* 2d Carroll & Graf ed. reprint (New York: Carroll & Graf, 1987), n.pag., Taylor has in fact said his goal is "to make each line on the page sound unlike either a line of prose or a line of poetry."

9. Taylor has revealed the real-life origins of three of these stories: "Three Heroines"—"almost literally what happened: an account of my going home, and my mother and the woman that had always looked after her" (Thompson, "Interview," 161); "Her Need"—speculation on the sight one morning in Charlottesville of "a young woman, thirty-five or so, with her teen-age son, . . . driving him somewhere" (ibid., 144); "The Hand of Emmagene"—a story heard fifteen years before about a human hand found mysteriously in a trash can (ibid., 144; Brickhouse, "Writing, Teaching," 52).

10. Anatole Broyard, review of *In the Miro District, New York Times Book Review,* 3 April 1977, 14.

11. Northrop Frye, *Anatomy of Criticism: Four Essays* (New York: Atheneum, 1970), 247.

12. Daniel, "Inspired Voice," 45.

13. "A Cheerful Disposition" is discussed in chapter 10.

14. Jonathan Yardley, "Peter Taylor: The Quiet Virtuoso," *Book World* [*Washington Post*], 27 January 1985, 3.

15. See, for instance, Melody Beattie, *Co-Dependent No More* (n.p.: Hazelden Foundation, 1987), and Wayne Kritsberg, *The Adult Children of Alcoholics Syndrome* (New York: Bantam Books, 1988).

16. McAlexander, "Composite Conversation," 126; Broadway, "Conversation," 89–90; Robison, "Interview," 144–45.

17. Steven John Ross, "Adapting 'The Old Forest' to Film," *Journal of the Short Story in English*, no. 9 (Autumn 1987):57–58.

18. W. Hampton Sides, "Interview: Peter Taylor," in *Conversations*, 136, 135.

Chapter Ten

1. Smith, "*PW* Interviews," 64.

2. Thompson, "Interview," 160.

3. Robert Towers, "A Master of the Miniature Novel," *New York Times Book Review*, 17 February 1985, 26.

4. Broadway, "Conversation," 77.

5. McAlexander, "Composite Conversation," 119.

6. Ibid., 126.

7. *A Summons to Memphis* (New York: Alfred A. Knopf, 1986), 194; hereafter cited as *STM*.

8. McAlexander, "Composite Conversation," 127.

9. Ibid.

10. Robert Towers, "Ways Down South," *New York Review of Books*, 25 September 1986, 57; Walter Sullivan, "The Last Agrarian: Peter Taylor Early and Late," *Sewanee Review* 95 (Spring 1987):317.

11. John Updike, "Summonses, Indictments, Extenuating Circumstances," *New Yorker*, 3 November 1986, 161–65.

12. "The Party," *River* 1 (March 1937):4–8, and "The Lady Is Civilized," *River* 1 (April 1937):50–54.

13. "The School Girl," *American Prefaces* 7 (Spring 1942):272–76.

14. "Attendant Evils," *Vanderbilt Miscellany, 1919–1944*, ed. Richmond Croom Beatty (Nashville: Vanderbilt University Press, 1944), 144–50.

15. "Uncles," *New Yorker*, 17 December 1949, 24–28.

16. Robison, "Interview," 144. See also J. H. E. Paine, "Interview with Peter Taylor," *Journal of the Short Story in English*, no. 9 (Autumn 1987):25, and Don Keck DuPree, "An Interview with Peter Taylor," in *Conversations*, 58.

17. "Nerves," *New Yorker*, 16 September 1961, 38–41.

18. Robison, "Interview," 143–44.

19. "A Cheerful Disposition," *Sewanee Review* 75 (Spring 1967):243–65; "Tom, Tell Him," *Sewanee Review* 76 (Spring 1968):159–86; "The End of Play," *Virginia Quarterly Review* 41 (Spring 1965): 248–65.

20. Paine, "Interview," 22.

21. "Peach Trees Gone Wild in the Lane," *Ploughshares* 2, no. 4 (1975):140; "The Megalopolitans," *Ploughshares* 2, no. 4 (1975):141–50; "Five Miles from Home," *Ploughshares* 5, no. 2 (1979):82–84; "Knowing," *Agenda* 13, no. 4, and 14, no 1. (combined issue, Winter/Spring 1976):97–100; "His Other Life," *Ploughshares* 2, no. 4 (1975):137–39, and *Agenda* 13, no. 4, and 14, no. 1 (combined issue, Winter/Spring, 1976):95–97.

22. Ashley Brown, "Peter Taylor at Sixty," *Shenandoah* 28, no. 2 (Winter 1977):53.

23. Robison, "Interview," 141. Taylor has also referred to this work by the titles *The Senator's Daughters* and *The Daughter of the Senator* (Paine, "Interview," 34).

24. Robert Penn Warren, "Two Peters: Memory and Opinion," *Shenandoah* 28, no. 2 (Winter 1977):9–10.

25. Louis D. Rubin, Jr., *The Faraway Country: Writers of the Modern South* (Seattle: University of Washington Press, 1963), 236–37.

26. Louise Y. Gossett, *Violence in Recent Southern Fiction* (Durham: Duke University Press, 1965), ix.

27. Welty, "Place in Fiction," 123.

28. *Literature, Sewanee,* [2].

29. William Peden, *The American Short Story* (Boston: Houghton Mifflin, 1964), 1.

30. Henry James, "Anthony Trollope," in *The Future of the Novel,* ed. Leon Edel (New York: Vintage Books, 1956), 259–60.

31. Walter Sullivan, "The Continuing Renascence: Southern Fiction in the Fifties," in *South: Modern Southern Literature in Its Cultural Setting,* ed. Louis D. Rubin, Jr., and Robert D. Jacobs (Garden City, N.Y.: Doubleday [Dolphin Books], 1961), 390.

32. *Literature, Sewanee,* [3].

33. James, "Anthony Trollope," 240.

34. Peden, *American Short Story,* 68.

35. *Literature, Sewanee,* [7].

Selected Bibliography

PRIMARY WORKS

Fiction and Drama

The Collected Stories of Peter Taylor. New York: Farrar, Straus, & Giroux, 1969. Includes "Dean of Men," "First Heat," "Reservations," "The Other Times," "At the Drugstore," "A Spinster's Tale," "The Fancy Woman," "Their Losses," "Two Pilgrims," "What You Hear from 'Em?" "A Wife of Nashville," "Cookie," "Venus, Cupid, Folly, and Time," "1939," "There," "The Elect," "Guests," "Heads of Houses," "Mrs. Billingsby's Wine," "*Je Suis Perdu,*" and "Miss Leonora When Last Seen."

Happy Families Are All Alike: A Collection of Stories. New York: McDowell, Obolensky, 1959. Includes "The Other Times," "Promise of Rain," "Venus, Cupid, Folly, and Time," "A Friend and Protector," "A Walled Garden," "The Little Cousins," "Guests," "1939," "*Je Suis Perdu,*" and "Heads of Houses."

In the Miro District and Other Stories. New York: Alfred A. Knopf, 1977. Includes "The Captain's Son," "The Instruction of a Mistress," "The Throughway," "The Hand of Emmagene," "Daphne's Lover," "Her Need," "Three Heroines," and "In the Miro District."

A Long Fourth and Other Stories. Introduction by Robert Penn Warren. New York: Harcourt, Brace, 1948. Includes "The Scoutmaster," "The Fancy Woman," "Allegiance," "Rain in the Heart," "Sky Line," "A Spinster's Tale," and "A Long Fourth."

Miss Leonora When Last Seen and Fifteen Other Stories. New York: Ivan Obolensky, 1963. Includes "Reservations," "An Overwhelming Question," "At the Drugstore," "Sky Line," "A Strange Story," "The Fancy Woman," "A Spinster's Tale," "Allegiance," *The Death of a Kinsman,* "Miss Leonora When Last Seen," "A Wife of Nashville," "What You Hear from 'Em?" "Two Pilgrims," "Their Losses," "Bad Dreams," and "Cookie."

The Old Forest and Other Stories. Garden City, N.Y.: Dial Press (Doubleday), 1985. Includes "The Gift of the Prodigal," "The Old Forest," "Promise of Rain," "Bad Dreams," "A Friend and Protector," "A Walled Garden," "Allegiance," "The Little Cousins," "A Long Fourth," "Rain in the Heart," "Porte Cochere," "The Scoutmaster," "Two Ladies in Retirement," and *The Death of a Kinsman.*

Presences: Seven Dramatic Pieces. Boston: Houghton Mifflin, 1973. Includes *Two Images, A Father and a Son, Missing Person, The Whistler, Arson, A Voice through the Door,* and *The Sweethearts.*

A Stand in the Mountains. New York: Frederic C. Beil, 1985. Drama.
A Summons to Memphis. New York: Alfred A. Knopf, 1986. Novel.
Tennessee Day in St. Louis: A Comedy. New York: Random House, 1957.
The Widows of Thornton. New York: Harcourt, Brace, 1954. Includes "Their Losses," "What You Hear from 'Em?" "Porte Cochere," "A Wife of Nashville," *The Death of a Kinsman,* "Cookie," "Two Ladies in Retirement," "Bad Dreams," and "The Dark Walk."
A Woman of Means. New York: Harcourt, Brace, 1950. Also: New York: Frederic C. Beil, 1983. Novel.

Nonfiction

"Acceptance by Peter Taylor." *Proceedings,* American Academy and Institute of Arts and Letters, 2d ser., no. 29 (1979):31–32. Remarks on receipt of Gold Medal for the short story 17 May 1978.
"A Commemorative Tribute to Jean Stafford." *Shenandoah* 30, no. 3 (Spring 1979):56–60. Also: *Proceedings,* American Academy and Institute of Arts and Letters, 2d ser., no. 30 (1980):79–85.
"Eudora Welty." In *Eudora Welty: A Tribute,* [31–32]. Winston-Salem: Printed for Stuart Wright, 1984.
Literature, Sewanee, and the World: Founder's Day Address 1972. Sewanee, Tenn.:University of the South, 1972. On occasion of receipt of D. Litt.
"Randall Jarrell." In *Randall Jarrell, 1914–1965,* edited by Robert Lowell, Peter Taylor, and Robert Penn Warren, 241–52. New York: Farrar, Straus, & Giroux, 1967. Earlier versions: "Tribute at Yale." *Alumni News* (University of North Carolina at Greensboro) 54 (Spring 1966):2–5. "That Cloistered Jazz." *Michigan Quarterly Review* 5 (Fall 1966):237–45.
"Reminiscences." In *The Fugitives, the Agrarians, and Other Twentieth Century Southern Writers,* 17–21. Charlottesville: Alderman Library, University of Virginia, 1985.
"Robert Traill Spence Lowell: 1917–1977." *Proceedings,* American Academy and Institute of Arts and Letters, 2d ser., no. 28 (1978):71–79. Also: *Ploughshares* 5, no. 2 (1979):74–81.
"Tennessee Caravan, 1920–1940." In *Tennessee: A Homecoming,* edited by John Netherton, 59–66. Nashville: Third National Corp., 1985. Childhood memoir.

Uncollected Fiction, Drama, and Poetry

"Attendant Evils." In *Vanderbilt Miscellany, 1919–1944,* edited by Richmond Croom Beatty, 144–50. Nashville: Vanderbilt University Press, 1944. Story.
"A Cheerful Disposition." *Sewanee Review* 75 (Spring 1967):243–65. Story.
The Early Guest. Shenandoah 24 (Winter 1973):21–43. Also published in a limited signed chapbook edition (Winston-Salem: Palaemon Press, 1982). "A sort of a

story, a sort of a play, a sort of a dream"—a synopsis in dramatic form of an abandoned novel.

"The End of Play." *Virginia Quarterly Review* 41 (Spring 1965):248–65. Story.

"Five Miles from Home." *Ploughshares* 5, no. 2 (1979):82–84. Verse narrative.

"The Furnishings of a House." *Kenyon Review* 1, no. 3 (Autumn 1939):308. Poem.

"His Other Life." *Ploughshares* 2, no. 4 (1975):137–39. Also: *Agenda* 13, no. 4, and 14, no. 1 (combined issue, Winter/Spring 1976):95–97. Verse narrative.

"Knowing." *Agenda* 13, no. 4, and 14, no. 1 (combined issue, Winter/Spring 1976):97–100. Verse narrative.

"The Lady Is Civilized." *River* 1 (April 1937):50–54. Story.

"The Megalopolitans." *Ploughshares* 2, no. 4 (1975):141–50. Verse narrative.

"Nerves." *New Yorker,* 16 September 1961, 38–41. Story.

"The Party." *River* 1 (March 1937):4–8. Story.

"Peach Trees Gone Wild in the Lane." *Ploughshares* 2, no. 4 (1975):140. Verse narrative.

"The School Girl." *American Prefaces* 8, no. 3 (Spring 1942):272–77. Story.

"Tom, Tell Him." *Sewanee Review* 76 (Spring 1968):159–86. Story.

"Uncles." *New Yorker,* 17 December 1949, 24–28. Story.

Miscellaneous

Interrupted Honeymoon. U. S. Steel Hour television adaptation of short story "Reservations." 6 September 1961.

The Old Forest. A sixty-minute color film by Stephen John Ross based on short story "The Old Forest." Narrated by Peter Taylor. Pyramid Films and Videos, 1985.

Three Heroines and *The Instruction of a Mistress.* Audiotape recording of two verse narratives, read by the author, Peter Taylor. Produced by New Letters on the Air. American Audio Prose Library, NL17.

SECONDARY WORKS

Bibliographies

Kramer, Victor A., Patricia A. Bailey, Carol G. Dana, and **Carl H. Griffin.** *Andrew Lytle, Walker Percy, and Peter Taylor: A Reference Guide.* Boston: G. K. Hall, 1983. Pages 185–243 on Taylor. Annotated list of articles, reviews, and other secondary material from 1948 to part of 1980, with introduction by Griffin and index; indispensable.

Wright, Stuart. *Peter Taylor: A Descriptive Bibliography, 1934–87.* Charlottesville: Bibliographic Society of the University of Virginia, by University of Virginia Press, 1988. Lists primary works only; all editions and reprints fully described, with variants noted.

Special Issues of Journals

Critique 9, no. 3 (1967). Featured articles by Barbara Schuler, "The House of Peter Taylor," 6–18, and James Penny Smith, "Narration and Theme in Taylor's *A Woman of Means*," 19–30, plus the first Taylor bibliography, "A Peter Taylor Checklist," 31–36, also by Smith.

Journal of the Short Story in English, no. 9 (Autumn 1987). Edited by J. H. E. Paine, who interviews Taylor; articles by Cleanth Brooks, Z. Vance Wilson, Steven John Ross, J. A. Bryant, Simone Vauthier, and Philip Hanson; plus a bibliographical checklist of primary works, 1934–86, by Stuart Wright.

Sewanee Review 70 (Autumn 1962). First publication of Taylor's "At the Drugstore," plus major articles by Morgan Blum, "Peter Taylor: Self-Limitation in Fiction," 559–78, Brainard Cheney, "Peter Taylor's Plays," 579–87, and Ashley Brown, "The Early Fiction of Peter Taylor," 588–602.

Shenandoah 78, no. 2 (Winter 1977). "A Garland for Peter Taylor on His Sixtieth Birthday"—poems by Robert Lowell and Richard Howard; reminiscences by Robert Penn Warren, Allan Tate, Andrew Lytle, Brainard Cheney, Mary Jarrell, David McDowell, Stephen Goodwin, Thomas Molyneux, John Casey, and Robert Wilson; appreciations by Herschel Gower, Ashley Brown, Albert J. Griffith, and J. F. Powers; and a parody by John Thompson.

Biographical Material

Binding, Paul. "Peter Taylor." In *Separate Country: A Literary Journey Through the American South*, 114–21. New York: Paddington Press, 1979. Sketch based on interview at University of Virginia.

Coffey, Shelby, III. "Sophisticated Fugitive: Peter Taylor and the *New Yorker*." *Potomac (Washington Post)*, 24 November 1968, 23, 28–30. Interview, with brief extract from aborted novel Taylor worked on in the 1970s.

Cowser, Robert G. "Peter Taylor and Trenton." In *River Region Monographs: Reports on People and Popular Culture*, edited by Neil Graves, 17–24. Martin: University of Tennessee at Martin, 1975. Anecdotes about the Taylor family.

Gareffa, Peter M., and **Jean Ross.** "Taylor, Peter (Hillsman) 1917– ." In *Contemporary Authors*, 487–91. New Revision Series, vol. 9. Detroit: Gale Research, 1983. Includes 1981 phone interview by Ross.

James, Caryn. "Some Southern Rascals." *New York Times Book Review*, 19 October 1986, 53. Capsule interview related to *A Summons to Memphis*.

Jones, Malcolm. "Mr. Peter Taylor When Last Seen." *Greensboro [N. C.] Daily News/Record*, 27 July 1980, C5. Personality interview.

Jordan, Jenice. "He 'Writes for Fun,' but His Stories Sell." *Columbus Dispatch*, 6 December 1959, book section. Very early interview, when Taylor was at Ohio State University.

Kernan, Michael. "Peter Taylor and the Layers of Life." *Washington Post*, 4 March 1985, B1, B6. Informative, wide-ranging interview.

Kramer, Victor A. "Peter Taylor." In *Dictionary of Literary Biography Yearbook 1981,* edited by Karen L. Rood, Jean W. Ross, and Richard Ziegfield, 256–60. Detroit: Gale Research, 1982. Excellent overview of Taylor's career.

McAlexander, Hubert H., ed. *Conversations with Peter Taylor.* Literary Conversations Series. Jackson: University Press of Mississippi, 1987. Fourteen interviews from 1960 to 1987, including information-packed conversations with Stephen Goodwin, J. William Broadway, Barbara Thompson, and McAlexander. The most valuable source of biographical information available; indispensable.

McDowell, Edwin. "At 69, Master Storyteller Wins New Recognition." *New York Times,* 7 May 1986. Phone interview about receipt of PEN/Faulkner award.

Morrow, Mark. "Peter Taylor." In *Images of the Southern Writer,* 78–79. Athens: University of Georgia Press, 1985. Brief interview with portrait.

"Taylor, Peter (Hillsman)." In *Current Biography Yearbook 1987,* edited by Charles Moritz, 552–56. New York: H. W. Wilson, 1988. Most up-to-date of reference book sketches.

Critical Studies

Brooks, Cleanth. "The Southern Temper." In *A Shaping Joy: Studies in the Writer's Craft,* 198–214. New York: Harcourt Brace Jovanovich, 1971. Discusses "Miss Leonora When Last Seen" as example of the Southern temper.

Casey, Jane Barnes. "A View of Peter Taylor's Stories." *Virginia Quarterly Review* 54 (Spring 1978):213–30. Analyzes seven stories in regard to Taylor's changing ideas about social order, especially male-female relationships.

Cathey, Kenneth Clay. "Peter Taylor: An Evaluation." *Western Review* 18, no. 1 (Autumn 1953):9–19. The first major critical appraisal; stresses Taylor's obvious promise, narrow range, and steady improvement.

Kazin, Alfred. *Bright Book of Life: American Novelists and Storytellers from Hemingway to Mailer.* Boston: Atlantic, Little, Brown, 1973. Three-page look at overall techniques.

Lytle, Andrew. "The Displaced Family." *Sewanee Review* 66 (Winter 1958):115–31. Thoughtful analysis of *Tennessee Day in St. Louis.*

Peden, William. "A Hard and Admirable Toughness: The Stories of Peter Taylor." *Hollins Critic* 7, no. 1 (February 1970):1–9. Examines social change and internal character conflicts in *Collected Stories.*

Pinkerton, Jan. "The Vagaries of Taste and Peter Taylor's 'A Spinster's Tale.'" *Kansas Quarterly* 9, no. 2 (Spring 1977):81–85. Discusses role of taste in critical evaluations.

Raskin, Barbara. "Southern Fried." *New Republic,* 18 October 1969, 29–30. Representative example of Taylor's rare negative reviews; sees *Collected Stories* as "mind-deadening"; finds Taylor's nostalgia for "frivolous, unimportant, superficial, silly, Southern whites" an indictment of both the author and his work.

Robinson, Clayton. "Peter Taylor." In *Literature of Tennessee,* edited by Ray

Willbanks, 149–61. Rome, Ga.: Mercer University Press, 1984. Stresses treatment of middle-class urban life.

Robinson, David. "Summons from the Past." *Southern Review* 23, no. 3 (Summer 1987):754–59. Reviews *A Summons to Memphis* as "a novel whose present is abstract and bloodless, while its past is richly realized."

———. "Tennessee, Taylor, the Critics, and Time." *Southern Review* 23, no. 2 (Spring 1987):281–94. Careful critique of "Venus, Cupid, Folly, and Time" as an enthralling psychological analysis.

Robison, James Curry. *Peter Taylor: A Study of the Short Fiction.* Twayne's Studies in Short Fiction. Boston: Twayne Publishers, 1988. Analyzes key stories from early, middle, and late periods; includes new interview by Robison, portions of two other interviews, extracts from eleven critics or other commentators, chronology, bibliography, and index.

Shear, Walter. "Peter Taylor's Fiction: The Encounter with the Other." *Southern Literary Journal* 21, no. 2 (Spring 1989):50–63. Argues that Taylor depicts characters' encounters with the other as leading to the discovery of the self's seemingly permanent relationship to society.

Smith, Ron. "Peter Taylor." In *Critical Survey of Short Fiction,* edited by Frank N. Magill, 6:2304–11. Englewood Cliffs, N.J.: Salem Press, 1981. Detailed analysis of "A Wife of Nashville," plus general comments on overall work.

Sodowsky, Roland, and **Gargi Roysircar Sodowsky.** "Determined Failure, Self-Styled Success: Two Views of Betsy in Peter Taylor's 'Spinster's Tale.'" *Studies in Short Fiction* 25, no. 1 (Winter 1988):49–54. Analyzes Freudian and Adlerian motifs.

Sullivan, Walter. "The Last Agrarian: Peter Taylor Early and Late." *Sewanee Review* 95 (Spring 1987):308–17. Excellent assessment of Taylor's work, as exemplified in four most recent books.

Warren, Robert Penn. Introduction to Peter Taylor, *A Long Fourth and Other Stories.* New York: Harcourt, Brace, 1948. Laudatory essay that launched Taylor's career and determined the issues and the tone for most later criticism.

Weaver, Gordon, ed. *The American Short Story 1945–1980: A Critical History.* Twayne's Critical History of the Short Story. Boston: Twayne Publishers, 1983. In different sections of the book, Jeffrey Walker, E. P. Walkiewicz, and James C. Robison comment on Taylor's work over three decades.

Williamson, Alan. "Identity and the Wider Eros: A Reading of Peter Taylor's Stories." *Shenandoah* 30, no. 1 (Fall 1978):71–84. Praises Taylor's affirmative comic themes dealing with Eros as a force of social cohesion.

York, Lamar. "Peter Taylor's Version of Initiation." *Mississippi Quarterly* 40, no. 3 (Summer 1987):309–22. Notes how Taylor deals with child's leaving family from point of view of the parent.

Young, Thomas Daniel. "The Contemporary Scene." In *Tennessee Writers,* 77–111. Knoxville: University of Tennessee Press, 1981. Good overview, with detailed analysis of "A Long Fourth."

Index